SRI SANKARACHARYA

SRI SANKARACHARYA

C. N. KRISHNASAMY AIYAR

GYAN

Published by

Gyan Publishing House
5, Ansari Road
Daryaganj, New Delhi-110002
Phone: 011-47034999, 9811692060
E-mail: books@gyanbooks.com

Distribution Network
gyanbooks.com
India, USA, Canada, UK, Australia

ISBN: 978-93-7169-110-9 (PB)

First Published, 1929

2nd Impression 2025

Printed at: Gyan Press, Delhi.

SRI SANKARACHARYA

Author: C. N. KRISHNASAMY AIYAR

SRI

SANKARACHARYA

I

HIS LIFE AND TIMES

BY

C. N. KRISHNASAMY AIYAR, M. A., L. T.,
Assistant, Native College, Coimbatore.

II

HIS PHILOSOPHY

BY

PANDIT SITANATH TATTVABHUSHAN,
Author of " Hindu Theism."

THIRD EDITION.

G. A. NATESAN & Co., ESPLANADE, MADRAS.

PREFACE TO THE FIRST EDITION.

WHEN any earnest and thoughtul student of human civilisation turns his attention to the study of the part which India has played in the development of man's humanity, he cannot fail to learn distinctly that the moral influence of Indian thought and life has been great, indeed, in determining and fixing those really noble spiritual elements of civilisation which constitute as it were, the foundation of that same humanity. The subtle manner in which even now Indian thought is spreading throughout the world is not only indicative of the power possessed by that thought, but is also an illustration of the sweetly silent penetrativeness which has specially characterised it throughout history. Indeed, the true vital point in the constitution of any civilisation is found out to be that through which it comes into contact with other civilisations so as to influence them well in their own growth and advancement. The essential vitality of a civilisation, so ascertained from the nature of the external effects produced by it, is also seen invariably to be the basis of the unity and continuity possessed by that civilisation. Judged in this manner, the soul of Hindu civilisation is at once made out to be in the religious history of India ; it is the religious philosophy of India that has both directly and indirectly influenced the civilisations of the East and West, and it is mainly in religious expansion and development that we see the continued progress and growth of Indian enlightenment. Therefore, the history of religion in India has a much larger meaning than it can have in connection with the civilisation of any other country or nationality.

In this religious history of India perhaps no one has, at any rate during the last one thousand years, played a more prominent part than Sankara, a connected account of whose life and teachings is presented briefly in English in this volume. It is hoped that the readers of this volume will find therein such materials of thought and history as will enable them to know accurately the position of Sankara in the evolution of the national religious life of the Hindu people, and enable them also at the same time to estimate correctly the great value of his work in life as viewed from the standpoint of history. How he was the product of the age in which he was born, how he in his turn impressed his personality on the unity of Hindu life and civilisation, how his work as a scholar and reformer has been in harmony with the historic genius of the

Hindu nation, and how, lastly, this work of his has, owing to this very harmony, become fully assimilated into the life of the living India of to-day are all things which are sure to strike the observant reader of Sankara's Life and Times. So far as we the people of this land are concerned, our very nearness to Sankara is apt to blind us to the larger features of his historic work and achievements; and to make these manifest, we may well quote here the estimate of Sankara as given by Sister Nivedita, a worthy English lady who has by the power of her sympathy beautifully succeeded in raising herself to a condition of consonance with Hindu ideals of life and its aims :—

> Western people can hardly imagine a personality like that of Sankaracharya. In the course of a few years to have nominated the founders of no less than ten great religious orders, of which four have fully retained their prestige to the present day; to have acquired such a mass of Sanskrit learning as to create a distinct philosophy and impress himself on the scholarly imagination of India is a pre-eminence that twelve hundred years have not sufficed to shake; to have written poems whose grandeur makes them unmistakable, even to foreign and unlearned ears; and at the same time to have lived with his disciples in all the radiant love and simple pathos of the saints—this is the greatness that we must appreciate but cannot understand. We contemplate with wonder and delight the devotion of Francis of Assisi, the intellect of Abelard, the virile force and freedom of Martin Luther, and the political efficiency of Ignatius Loyola; but who could imagine all these united in one person?

It may appear to some that this estimate is too favourably coloured; but we wish to remind such persons that in the very combination of these variedly heroic characteristics there is a factor which has a natural tendency to tone down the pointedness of each of the many aspects of Sankara's many-sided greatness and heroism. If this little book does in any way help on a proper appreciation of such a historic personage as the great Sankara, all those that have taken part in its preparation and publication will feel quite abundantly rewarded; for, India suffers to-day in the estimation of the world more through that world's ignorance of the achievements of the heroes of Indian history than through the absence or the insignificance of such achievements.

CONTENTS.

I
Life and Times of Sankara.

CHAPTER VI.

PAGE

THE WORK OF SANKARA.

II.

The Philosophy of Sankaracharya.

LIFE AND TIMES OF SANKARA.

CHAPTER I.

INTRODUCTION.

1. SOURCES OF INFORMATION AND THEIR VALUE.

"AS far as it is known," says a recent American writer in speaking of the great Athenian Sage, "the life of Socrates, in its merely outward bodily incident, may be told in a paragraph." Such, it is to be feared, is also the case with Sankara, whose life it is here purposed to sketch. Few of the facts of his life can be narrated with certainty, not even the time and the place of his birth.

Yet the need for a reliable and historic account of Sankara is being felt more and more; for, the Adwaita Philosopby, of which he was the foremost expounder and which has since his time enjoyed a wide and more or less steady popularity throughout India, has latterly had additional importance given to it by the Vedantic studies of Western scholars, European and American, and by the spread of Theosophic thought. The comparative method is being applied to it and its merit is being thus tested. Christian and other hostile sects seek to expose what they believe to be its shortcomings. This intelligent study of Sankara's works has naturally aroused a desire to ascertain the facts of the 'external' life of the Teacher. As yet, however, but few really historic memoirs exist of the life and times of Sankara, written in a true historic spirit and with the object of showing him just as he was. The aim of the present sketch is accordingly to gather together for the benefit of the general reader what is to be found in the *Sankaravijayas* or 'Triumphs of Sankara' which have come down to us, and in the monographs and stray items of information available in the recent writings of modern enquirers.

These 'original authorities' are—(1) the *Sankaravijayas* of Madhavacharya, Anandagiri, Chidvilasa and Swami Sadananda, arranged perhaps in chronological order here; (2) a chapter which is to be found in the ninth *Amsa of Skanda Purana;* and (3) *Madhvavijaya* and *Manimanjari*, both by Pandit Narayanacharya, a hostile Mâdhva writer. And of recent writers, Wilson, Max Müller, and Telang may be mentioned as the most important. A few words regarding the relative merits of these several sources are needed to prevent misconceptions and explain the attitude of the present writer towards them.

Madhavacharya, whose work is placed first in the list, is the well-known Vidyaranya, who was minister of Hukka and Bukka, Kings of Vijayanagar, and became later on the chief of the Sringeri Mutt. This fact settles the time when this *Sankaravijaya* was written, whether Vidyaranya wrote it himself or caused it to be written by some one else; for, considered as a literary effort, it is to be feared that, matter and manner taken together, the work does not reflect much credit on the critical capacity and historic judgment of the author. It is quite clear from internal evidence that it was meant to be a counterblast to the Mâdhva writings above mentioned. Of the other *Sankara-vijayas*, it need only be said that they all show traces of relatively later origin, though Wilson claims for Anandagiri age as well as trustworthiness. This, however, Telang has shown to be groundless and untenable. The chapter of *Skandapurana* has been mentioned only to show that it is a very recent and poor interpolation and has even less historic value. *Madhvavijaya* and *Manimanjari* are, on the other hand, owing to their nature, very interesting for historic purposes. In his sketch of the life of Madhva, the writer of this account has endeavoured to show that these works were the fruit of the persecution which that teacher of dualistic Vedanta had received from the then incumbents of the Sringeri Mutt, and that he had on that account been forced to call himself Bhima, and make Sankara, one of whose successors at the *Sringeri* Mutt accidentally bearing the same name, (as has been shown elsewhere), had been troubling him, an *avatar* of a Rakshasa, Maniman by name, mentioned in the *Mahabharata.* Pandit Narayana, one of the followers of Madhva, in the next generation, put these hints together along with some traditions current in Malabar about Sankara, and thus composed these two works of his, with intent to discredit Sankara's origin and his doctrines.

2. Hinduism before Sankara: Buddhism.

The life of Sankara, like that of every other great man, has to begin with the description of the state of things in the midst of which he was born and brought up, for "each man, poet or philosopher, inhales much before he exhales." Accordingly we have to consider the state of Hinduism at the time of the advent of this great Guru, and pass in rapid review the stages it had gone through before reaching that particular state.

It is enough, however, to start with the period, whenever it was, when Vedic sacrifices constituted mainly the creed of Hinduism. In the words of the poet "kings (in those days) had milked the earth for sacrifices, and Indra, in return, the heavens, to help harvests on." There was the sacrifice of the horse, there was the sacrifice of the goat, and of all other things imaginable. And sacrifices had increased not merely in number but also in elaboration of ritual. Extravagant rewards had been promised by the promoters, which, however, could not be realised in practice and the unconvincing explanations invented to explain these failures away, merely served to hasten the fall of the system. Under such circumstances, therefore, the desire for inner religious improvement was slowly growing and making itself manifest. The opponents of animal sacrifices were to be found not merely among the Kshatriyas, but the more thoughtful among the Brahmins had also begun to sing the praises of divine contemplation and practical moral virtues, as against the extravagances of sacrifices. The *Upanishads* or "the top-knots of the *Vedas*" as they are sometimes termed, are almost everywhere of this line of thought, and one glorious hymn, chanted to this day by the orthodox *Smarta* Brahmin before breaking his fast, discovers in beautiful terms the meaning of the whole movement. It is known as आत्मयज्ञ (Sacrifice of the Self) and is well worthy of translation; but it being rather long, this sample will suffice for our present purpose:—"And of the sacrifice performed by the master who has understood these truths, the soul is the performer; the heart, the seat of the sacrificial fire; sensual desires, the ghee; anger, the sacrificial lamb; contemplation, fire; *the period of sacrifice, as long as life lasts*; whatever is eaten, is sacrificial rice; whatever is drunk, is the *soma* drink; and *death is the sacred bath concluding the ceremony*!"

This spirit, fostered by men of thought and encouraged by men of action over a long period, at last practically manifested itself in the teaching of Gautama, the Buddha. Most Hindus have learned to regard this teacher as an *avatar* of Vishnu, though strangely enough he is said to have come down not to establish religion and law by protecting the good and punishing the wicked, which is the mission of all the other *avatars* of Vishnu, but to delude some pious devotees of Siva as well as of Vishnu. Many others, who have learned to look upon him with better and more rational feelings, yet seem to regard him as an alien, and his faith as absolutely alien to India. This, it need hardly be pointed out, is a gross misreading of history. The teaching of Gautama, a member of a Rajput clan, was but a developed form of the thoughts and theories found in the *Upanishads*, with the freshness and vigour of his own personality and zeal added to them. The rapid spread of Buddhism among all classes is proof that he had 'set to music' just 'the tune which had been haunting millions of ears.' Long after his departure and after his inclusion in the Hindu Pantheon, Buddha's real service to mankind is described by Jayadeva, in one of his popular songs, to have been the propagation of the spirit of mercy and the abolition of animal sacrifices. For sings he, "O Thou of merciful heart! Thou didst condemn the slaughter of lambs at sacrifices, though enjoined by Srutis, when Thou didst take the shape of Buddha." His crusade against the killing of animals, and his battles so earnestly fought in favour of righteousness and renunciation, his use of the vernaculars in religious teaching instead of Sanskrit, and his organisation of bands of monks and nuns of all castes to spread his faith—all these points explain the electric speed with which Buddhism spread in his days as well as in the succeeding times, not merely over all parts of India but over vaster regions East and West.

Starting under such favourable conditions, however, this religion, like every other institution ever started by human agency, silently went on changing from century to century, and during its later life became corrupt in many ways. Gross idolatry in practice (c.f. Hiouen Tsang), formal atheism in doctrine, a regular army of monks and nuns everywhere eating up the substance of the industrious and charged with the worst evils of decayed monasticism, were only a few of its bad features. Its enemies, the Brahmins, at length felt that the time had come for them to use the logic and rhetoric of Buddhists against themselves,—and they began to do it effectively.

3. Revived Hinduism: Its Defects.

Among these neo-Hindu missionaries, Kumarila Bhatta is evidently the most renowned. Tradition connects him with a fierce and relentless conflict against the Buddhist, of which more will be said later on. Here it is enough to note that his peculiar faith was in what is known as *Karma-marga*, that is, salvation by the sole means of the faithful performance of *Karmas* or the daily and other periodical ceremonial rites enjoyed by the *Vedas* and the *Smritis*. His success, whatever it was, was due, not certainly to the advocacy of animal sacrifices, whose day had most assuredly fled, and to which mere lip-service was all that anybody would render, but to the revival of the harmless rites, made more impressive and more authoritative through his successfully meeting the arguments of the Buddhists against the

Vedic religion and in favour of their own faith.

Bhatta's was only one of the many sects that had been formed at various times in the later progress of Hinduism. There were *Bhairavas, Saktas, Ganapatyas*, with many sub-divisions among each; and the name of these sects was really legion.* They had all based their faiths, however, on the Vedas; particular texts or passages, torn from the context and specially interpreted, formed their scripture; and several of them had begun to claim greater authority for the *Puranas* or the *Smritis* on which they had based their belief, than even that which belonged to the *Vedas*. And, what was of infinitely greater importance, the *practices* of some of these religious sects were abominable or terrible. And every sect was intolerant of every other. The long and ceaseless wranglings of these sects

---

* शाक्यैः पाशुपतैरपि क्षपणकैः कापालिकैर्वैष्णवैरप्यन्यैरखिलैः खलैः खलुखिलं दुर्वादिभिर्वैदिकं पन्थानं परिरक्षितुं क्षितितलं प्राप्तः परिक्रीडते ॥

Sankara-vijaya.

and their occasional mutual persecutions and other hardships thereby caused had, at length, resulted in a general sense of weariness which seemed to have come over men, and an earnest hankering after some kind of harmonising principles, and general religious peace. Union and friendliness were possible only when a common basis could be so fashioned as to be comprehensive and able to allow for large differences of secondary importance, philosophically as well as practically. This then was assuredly the kind of unifying influence that was urgently needed. It was given to Sankara to supply this need, in the most wonderful manner possible and with the most solid success, and make *Vedanta* the basis of every religious sect that India has known, so as to satisfy the needs of men of all shades of intelligence and bias.

CHAPTER II.

BIRTH AND EARLY YEARS.

THE TIME AND PLACE OF HIS BIRTH.

An obscure village named Kaladi, six miles to the east of Alvoi, now a station on the Cochin-Shoranur Railway line, is traditionally mentioned as the birthplace of Sankara. It is not undisputed; for, Anandagiri mentions that place as Chidambaram. He is, however, alone in this statement. Further, the writer of *Manimanjari* gives it as Kaladi, and his testimony in such matters must be held peculiarly valuable for very obvious reasons. Again *Pazurpanai Illam*, one of the Nambudri families in the neighbourhood of Trichur, has been in all Malabar understood to be the family to which the mother of Sankara belonged, and her cremation ground thereabout is still shown to the enquirer as a place of interest. There is likewise a curious practice connected with the temple of Narayana at Badarikasrama on the Himalayas. The officiating priest there has been a Nambudri from Malabar for a long period, and the memory of no man goes back to a period when he was otherwise. And, as tradition assigns the founding of this temple to Sankara, the presence of the Nambudri there can easily be explained by his kinship to the founder. We have, therefore, every reason to believe that Sankara belonged to Malabar and to the Nambudri class of Brahmins.

The *Agrahara* of Kaladi is said to have been founded by a neighbouring chief, who was called Rajasekhara, if that be, indeed, a proper name. This chief dreamed, as thousands of other men have done, that Siva had become manifest in the neighbourhood of his capital in a spontaneously risen *Linga*. And he accordingly caused a temple to be built for the God and founded an *Agrahara* or settlement of Brahmins for the service of the temple. Among these was one of the name of Vidyadhiraja, which is evidently a title indicating his learning. He had an only son of the name of Sivaguru. They went through the usual course of instruction open in those days to Brahmin boys; and, having completed his studies, he married at the proper age and settled down as a householder. For a long time he was childless, and both husband and wife prayed to Siva to bless them with a son. At length, in consequence, as the *Sankaravijaya* puts it, of a plan agreed upon at Kailas between Siva and the Gods who had called there to learn how He was going to revive Hinduism, the God was pleased to bless the wife of Sivaguru and she became the mother of Sankara.

It would be a marvel if, in the case of such a great Guru like Sankara, as in so many other cases, later generations had found nothing extraordinary about his birth. Accordingly, in addition to the divine blessing noted just now, we have several other versions to consider in regard to the circumstances of the Guru's birth and parentage. Madhava adds that, before blessing Sivaguru's wife, the God asked her in a vision while she was asleep, whether she would have a number of dunces and ruffians for children, or an only wise son who was destined to be short-lived. She wisely chose the latter alternative, and had Sankara for her son.

Anandagiri, however, relates the story in an entirely different manner. We have seen that he mentions the place of Sankara's nativity as Chidambaram. We are told that there was a pious Brahmin living with his wife at this place, and that at one time the husband retired to a neighbouring forest after renouncing the world, that the wife continued for a long time to serve the Lord of Chidambaram, and that, as a reward of her devotion, the Lord was pleased to make her conceive in some mysterious and miraculous manner. And the child thus born to her was Sankara.

There is again another version of the story of Sankara's birth which we have to examine before we pass on. The writer of *Manimanjari* states that a Brahmin widow of Kaladi went astray from the ascetic life imposed upon her and begot a male child, and that this child was Sankara. This plain statement, however, is based on a tradition still current in some parts of Malabar, that a young widow of Kaladi once went to the temple of Siva along with other girls of her own age, and that, as some among them prayed for children, she also did so, that the Lord granted her request, and that she bore Sankara in consequence. The difficulties which Sankara is said to have experienced later on, in conducting the funeral rites of his mother, would also seem to confirm the suspicions about the illegitimacy of his birth, though the objections of his relatives were merely against *a Sanyasin* attempting to violate the rules of his order, by undertaking to perform the funeral rites of his dead mother.

We have no materials to enable us, at this distance of time, to estimate authoritatively the meaning of these stories regarding Sankara's birth. We see, however, that Madhava's book makes absolutely no mention whatever of these damaging traditions. If he had had any knowledge of or belief in them, he would surely not have left them unexplained; for, he has sought to explain away the other calumnies against Sankara as, for instance, the incidents relating to Bharati which will be mentioned later on. Further, there is a fairly strong argument to prove that all this talk about his birth being suspicious is unfounded. Both at the time of his renunciation and in connection with the funeral rites of his mother, we shall see that Sankara showed an extraordinary affection for her; in the latter case, he even went the length of offending the whole circle of his orthodox relations for the purpose of satisfying his mother's wishes. Now, as it has been a maxim with the Aryan Hindus to regard the unchaste mother, the indebted father and the idiotic son, as among the worst enemies of a man, Sankara would hardly have cared to suffer all the troubles and annoyances that he did on his mother's account, if she had not deserved that amount of sacrifice and filial love on his part, even when such sacrifice was unnecessary according to the strict letter of the law.

Accordingly, we may ascribe the whole of this tradition partially to calumny and partially to misguided admiration. It is also considered by some, we may add, that he was perhaps a posthumous son, and it is just possible that this simple fact was afterwards developed by friends no less than enemies on the lines of the mysterious with the most varied and grotesque results in every case.

If these are the difficulties in regard to the ascertainment of the place and the circumstances of Sankara's birth, infinitely greater are those that we have to face in trying to ascertain the time of his birth. The exact year of his birth is perhaps lost to us for ever, for, the horoscope given in Madhava's book is a mere imitation of Rama's and is, therefore, worthless.* The Sringeri Mutt, undoubtedly of the Guru's founding, has a list of his successors; but, unhappily, it is an imperfect

* Two views are generally held as to the probable time of the Guru's advent; namely, 788 A.D., which is accepted by one school of thinkers, and the close of the 6th century which is held by the other. It need hardly be observed that nothing *conclusive* has been arrived at by either party, nor is it likely to be until better data become available.

list, for besides other errors, it assigns to Suresvaracharya, the immediate successor of the Guru, a period of 700 years or more! Still as the time of this monk's birth is placed at the close of the eighth century of the Vikrama era, if we make some allowance for somebody's carelessness herein, it is easy perhaps to reconcile small discrepancies and take 788 A.D., as the year of the Guru's birth, as Max Müller does.

Two additional reasons would also seem to support this. Madhava's book locates the Buddhists mainly in Kashmir or more generally in the Himalayan regions; and Magadha does not seem to have figured in Sankara's days as the stronghold of Buddhism, or even as a province where the Buddhist were numerous, though in the minority. Now as Hiouen Tsang had found in the middle of the seventh century that Magadha was still dominantly Buddhistic under Siladitya II., a period of about 150 years is not too long for the decline of Buddhism in this province. Again, if the date assigned by the late Professor Sundaram Pillay to Sambandha could be accepted as the right and proper date, and if the allusion said to be found in one of Sankara's devotional songs is a real reference to that Tamilian saint, then the year that we have accepted has every probability of being the right date. As it is, however, it can only be regarded as provisional.

Telang, it must be noted, very ably pleads that Sankara must have been born somewhere towards the close of the sixth century, from a remarkable allusion in his *Sutra-Bhashya* to a Purna Varman, who was a Bhuddhistic King of Magadha at about that time. To the present writer, however, it seems to need additional and more direct evidence before that date may well be said to have been established. For the present, then, we proceed on the supposition that 788 A.D. indicates the year of Sankara's birth.

2. Early Years and Education.

The boy's early years were spent in the usual way. He was initiated into the mysteries of the alphabet at the proper time, and soon manifested uncommon intelligence. In his seventh year he was about to be invested with the sacred string, when his father died. His mother had the ceremony conducted later, and sent him to learn the *Vedas* and the *Vedangas*—from whom, we are not told. As has been said of several others, it is also said of Sankara that he learned all the *Vedas* and *Sastras* in two or three years—by the eigth year of his age he had finished his course of studies ! And the same writer who tells us this also informs us, almost in the same breath, that after his return from his Guru's home, where he had been staying for some years, fathers who had daughters to marry were anxious to offer them in marriage to him. Now, it is absolutely unheard of among Nambudris, at any time in their history, that a boy was married about his eigth year. One or the other of these statements, therefore, has to be rejected; and we may regard the tender age when he finished his course of studies as having been given in a careless manner or with intent to add to the Guru's greatness. We shall, therefore, reject it and hold that, in all probability, Sankara had become a young man by the time he returned to his own house, having, in the usual course, completed his study of the *Sastras* in the house and under the guidance of his teacher. This, however, is not meant to urge that there was nothing extraordinary about him. It only rejects tenth-rate and meaningless miracles. How capacious his mind was and how solid and how well the seeds of learning now sown in him blossomed forth when the time came for it, appears in every line of the commentaries, as will be shown later on.

Sankara's student-life being over, proposals of marriage began to be seriously entertained; and his mother must have been, as usual, busy consulting astrologers about the horoscopes of suitable girls. One day, about this time, we are told that the sage Agastya and other sages called at Sankara's house; and the talk turning on the length of his life, Agastya reminded the mother of her choice of a wise but short-lived son, and told her that her son was accordingly destined to die at an early age. All the story about the shortness of Sankara's life naturally looks very much like a prediction after the event. Accidents have often helped to guide innate tendencies and some accident, at this time, might have contributed to the sudden turn in Sankara's life. Whatever the reason, he seems immediately afterwards to have formed within himself a resolution to renounce the world and become a *Sanyasin*. Thus the talk of marriage was soon thrown into the background by his serious proposal to become at once a *Sanyasin*. The mother, as is usual in all similar cases, bewailed her sad fate, her loneliness during the remainder of her life, and felt sorry that there was to be no one to perform her funeral rites after her death. The *Sastras* declare that a *Sanyasin* is above all rites and ceremonies, so that even the performance of the funeral rites of his parents ceases to be obligatory on him. Sankara assured his mother, however, that, *Sanyasin* or no *Sanyasin*, he would always be ready to attend to her spiritual requirements. Even then his mother was not satisfied, and Sankara was obviously waiting for his opportunity in patience.

One day mother and son went to have their bath in the river. It was then in floods; and as he was having his plunge, he felt that a crocodile was pulling him by the foot. At once he shouted out to his mother in a loud voice,—"I am gone, dear mother! The crocodile is dragging me down. Let me have the satisfaction of dying a *Sanyasin*. Give me the permission needed. I shall then die in peace!" The mother in this crisis could not, of course, hesitate and at once told him that he was a *Sanyasin*.

Perhaps there was a real peril, and Sankara secured what is known as आपत्सन्यसन or the adoption of the vow of asceticism and mendicancy when death is near. However it was, he emerged from the water a declared *Sanyasin*. He repeated his promise to his mother, placed her under the care of his relatives, to whom he likewise left all his property, and left Kaladi in search of a Guru with a view to get himself *formally* initiated into the holy order of Hindu *Sanyasa*.

3. Renunciation.

In almost every part of India there have been recognised seats of Hindu learning sanctified through their association with the names of some great teachers. All the various branches of Ancient Indian learning have had their recognised founders and 'traditional' leaders. The *Vedanta-Sutras* of Badarayana, the *Karma-Sutras* of Jaimini and all other works of that kind have been taken up by particular 'schools' in various parts of the country, and their traditional interpretations of religious doctrine and philosophy have been treasured up and handed down by oral teaching to generations of earnest and faithful students. Of such seats of learning, Sankara was led to choose one 'on the bank of the Narmada'—evidently a hermitage—presided over at this time by a great *Sanyasin* of the name of Govinda. His teacher and perhaps also predecessor in office there was the famous Gaudapada. Hardly anything more has come down to us of Govinda than that he taught Sankara the germs of his philosophy. But as we find that, in every work that Sankara has left behind, he subscribes himself reverentially as the disciple of Sri Govinda Bhagavatpada, we may well take it to prove the great esteem that Sankara had for this teacher, as also the desire to publish his obligations to the teacher. Sankara also pays his respects to his *Parama-Guru*—*i.e.*, the teacher's teacher—Gaudapada, thus making it almost certain that the latter had just preceded Govinda.

The description of the first meeting of Govinda and his pupil is given both by Madhava and Chidvilasa. The former is perhaps at his worst here; for he makes Sankara go to the hermitage, cast himself at the teacher's feet, and on being asked who he was, answer—"Master, I am neither fire, nor air, nor earth, nor water—none of these, but the Supreme Spirit shining underneath all phenomena." In other words, he talks *Advaita* long before learning it! Chidvilasa locates the hermitage on the Himalayas; Sankara goes to Govinda there and pays his respects; and on being asked who he was, says—"I am the son of Sivaguru, a Brahmin of Kerala. My father died in my childhood, and I was brought up by my mother. I have had a fair course of training in the *Sastras.*" Then he goes on to give the crocodile incident already referred to, and requests the teacher to *formally* initiate him and invest him with the robe of the *Sanyasin.* Perhaps the temple at Badari was built in memory of these days.

Satisfied with this account, Govinda received this pupil with pleasure, and having made him go through the formalities needed, made him into a full *Sanyasin* and began to teach him the philosophy that he had himself learnt from Gaudapada. How long the course of discipline and instruction lasted we cannot tell. but it must have been a fairly long one. For, soon after its completion, Sankara leaves the hermitage and goes to Benares, where he receives pupils himself and begins to write his works and propagate his philosophy. It is said that Govinda desired Sankara to go to Benares first, and afterwards became one of those peripatetic teachers of religion who abounded so largely in pre-Buddhistic as well as post-Buddhistic India. To this day his name is invoked by his affectionate disciples as 'the best of peripatetic Teachers.'

CHAPTER III.

PREPARATION FOR THE GREAT MISSION.

I. Life at Benares. The Commentaries and other Works.

Accordingly Sankara went to Benares, and in that centre of learning soon distinguished himself in dialectics and philosophy, and began to attract pupils from various quarters. Among these was a young Brahmin from the land of the Cholas, *i. e.*, from Chidambaram or some part of what is now the District of Tanjore. He was admitted as a novice with the name of Padmapada, and his devotion to the *Guru* was unbounded. He, therefore, became specially endeared to him; and this having roused some impatience in the minds of the other disciples, Sankara, on one occasion, put his favourite's faith to the test in their presence by making him walk across the Ganges as if on solid ground, which he is said to have done because he had possessed the mustard seed of faith which moves mountains. We shall learn more, later on, of his unbounded faith in his master.

The order in which he wrote his works is not known to us; but judging from analogy, it is clear he must have attempted small things before beginning great ones. There is a tradition that he began with commenting on the Thousand Names of Vishnu (*Vishnu-Sahasra-nama*), and there is nothing improbable in it. The reader will easily find in his terse and beautiful explanations of these Names an earnest of what was to follow. Many small works of various kinds must have been written by him before he proceeded to comment on the chief *Upanishads*, or on the *Gita*, or, finally, on the *Vedanta-Sutras*. The commentary on the *Gita*, is said to betray some amount of impatience in regard to those who object to an unmarried young man turning out a *Sanyasin*. If it does, it must be evidently the expression of his personal feelings. There were likewise many original monographs composed at intervals as occasion called them forth. One such might be noted as a sample. One day Sankara was going along the street with his pupils to have his mid-day bath in the Ganges. A *Chandala* with his dogs was passing by him, when the pupils shouted to ask him to clear the road, as Brahmins do in Malabar to this day. The man, however, turned about and asked the *Guru* how he might consistently teach *Advaitism* and practice such differentiating observances. The *Guru* was struck by the answer, and its pertinency to the occasion called forth the five beautiful slokas forming the *Manisha Panchaka*, every one of which ends thus :—" He who has learned to look on phenomena in this (monistic) light is my true *Guru*, be he a *Chandala* or a twice-born man. This is my conviction." How the *Chandala* was able to address Sankara thus we are not told, but all difficulties in the situation are avoided by making him Siva in disguise. Another and one of the most popular of the *Guru's* minor songs is said to have had a similar origin. It is a poem of about twelve slokas whose refrain is—"Worship Govinda, worship Govinda, worship Govinda, O fool! When thou art face to face with Death at the appointed time, it is not the repetition of a grammatical formula that will save thee." The story is that he observed at Benares a student enthusiastically engaged in learning Sanskrit Grammar, and that, with the object of teaching him the futility of such studies in the matter of the salvation of the soul, the great *Guru* spontaneously burst out in song and gave vent to one of the most popular and musical of his smaller poems, which is even to-day very largely used as a devotional song almost all over India.

In this manner Sankara lived for several years at Benares, and sometimes at Badari to be free from bustle and disturbance, composing his works, submitting them to the wise men of his acquaintance in those parts and developing and revising them in the light of criticisms and controversies. Vyasa himself, the reputed author of the *Vedanta-Sutras*, is said to have on one occasion come to Sankara's abode as an old man; and, learning there from his pupils that he had commented on the *Vedanta-Sutras* Vyasa entered into a disputation with him on some knotty point; and this went on for a whole week, till Padmapada finding neither side disposed to give way, interposed and prayed that the *Avatars* of Vishnu and Siva might desist from further controversy and give the world peace! This, being interpreted, probably means that there was a good deal of wrangling over portions of Sankara's commentary on the *Vedanta-Sutras*, and that he was perhaps occasionally forced to give up some of his earlier positions and meet opponents half-way. The old man here might well represent an opponent of that kind, whom Sankara could not find it quite easy to satisfy and whose acquaintance with the literature of the *Vedanta* philosophy must have been so good as to entitle him to be looked upon as a re-incarnated Vyasa. The cardinal points, however, had now become settled and fortified and Sankara stood forth as the most uncompromising Monistic Teacher of India expounding in inimitable language, the great truth, of the familiar formula तत्वमसि, 'That thou art.'

2. Commencement of the Triumphal Tour.

The most important works of the Guru having thus been finished and tested and taught to his pupils, Sankara left Benares accompanied by a large number of his pupils and with a large collection of books. Chid-vilasa mentions the name of a certain Ratan Singh as the then chief of Benares, who, on this occasion, pressed Sankara to stay on with him. The Guru excused himself by saying that he had been asked by his master to be a peripatetic teacher, and that, therefore, his mission was to teach and preach over the whole of India. Perhaps this name of the then King of Benares is not of much value for historical purposes. But, aware as we are of the part played by royal patrons in those days in promulgating religion and in encouraging literature and philosophy, we need not doubt that Sankara's fame and influence began to spread by reason of the help rendered by royal chiefs and princes everywhere, no less than by his own worth; for, Anandagiri and Chidvilasa both agree in saying that the teacher had while on tour all the usual paraphernalia which the religious chiefs of Mutts display in our own days, and these could only have been gifts made by kings to Sankara in recognition of his religious learning and authority.

So, helped by the local chief of Benares, Sankara began his triumphal progress as a teacher. He must have been then over twenty-five years of age, if our supposition is correct regarding his age at the time when he became a *Sanyasin*. He first stopped at Prayag (Allahabad) and bathed at the confluence of the Jumna and the Ganges, and in his prayers remembered his parents. Afterwards, while he was resting in the shade of trees along the river bank with his disciples, news was brought to him that the great Bhatta, the champion of the *Purva-Mimamsa* school and the extirpator of North Indian Buddhism was about to commit himself to flames!

3. The Episode of Kumarila Bhatta.

This is the place to speak at some length of the life and doings of this historic personage. We have already had occasion to get a glance of his life-work, but we shall now pause to take a fuller view of him. He is believed to have been an Assamese Brahmin by some, while others profess to see in his *Vartika* conclusive proof of his connection with the land of Tamil, and the following account is mainly taken from what Madhava says of him. He went through the course of studies open to every Brahmin boy. But either his own inclinations, or motives such as are known to have influenced Christian missionaries like Father Beschi, led him soon to put on the disguise of a Buddhist and learn Buddhistic theology from a great teacher of Buddhism. For a time all went on well; but on one occasion this teacher in his discourse happened to be more severe than usual in ridiculing the divinity and the sanctity of the Vedas, so much so that Bhatta shed tears in consequence of it. His brother students who were all Buddhists, observed it and inferred that he must be a heretic. Accordingly, 'these pious people who had taken on themselves the vow never to harm animal life,' resolved that rather than suffer him to go abroad in possession of their secret doctrines and the weak points of their philosophy and turn their logic against themselves, they would do away with him altogether. So one night, as they were all chatting on the terrace of the Buddhist teacher's house, they contrived to trip him up, and down fell Kumarila exclaiming in a loud voice—"If it be true that the *Vedas* form the true Revelation, may they save me from harm!" He reached the ground safe enough, having lost but one of his eyes, which loss, we are told, was due to the doubt implied in the expression, '*If* it be true!' He somehow escaped with his life, and from that moment became the most uncompromising opponent of the Buddhistic faith and made it his mission to carry on a ruthless war of controversy against its followers. We have, however, only the account of what he did at the court of King Sudhanvan, though incidentally we are told that he had visited many other courts before arriving there. Here ensued a mighty controversy between the Buddhistic teachers at the king's court (the king was a Buddhist himself) and Bhatta, the uproar and din caused by which is said to have agitated the very heavens! Bhatta exposed their follies and their weak points with pitiless logic, and battered all their strongholds and defeated the enemy everywhere. Then he explained to the king his chief doctrines—that the *Vedas* were true and revealed verbally even as they are, and that they, therefore, formed the best proof of their own authority as well as the touchstone of the authority of the *Smritis*, *Puranas* and other scriptural works. स्वतः प्रमाणं परतः प्रमाणम्। He held that the earlier part of the *Vedas* relating to the sacrifice was alone capable of saving men, so that the really religious part of life according to him was to go through the rites enjoined in the sacrificial *Kanda* or section of the *Vedas*. But the king's turn for abstract reasoning was apparently only of indifferent excellence, and so he bluntly said :—"In matters of dialectics, success depends on the amount of one's knowledge and the length of one's tongue; and I, therefore, declare that I shall hold the faith of that man among you to be true and enduring, who casting himself from the top of the adjacent hill, remains whole!" Hereupon the Buddhists merely kept looking at each other, but the Brahmin readily undertook to risk his person. The ordeal was accordingly gone through in the presence of a large crowd, and Bhatta threw himself down with the exclamation already given and reached the ground 'like a pillow stuffed with down.' The Buddhists, however, argued that it was not the proper test in settling the truth of faiths, for the body in such cases could be protected from harm by means of drugs or charms or *yogic* practices. The king was wroth and proposed a second test as a kind of ultimatum. He caused a jar to be brought into the assembly with its mouth carefully covered and sealed, and said that he would espouse the faith of that party which could say truly what was inside the closed jar. The parties met next morning and the Buddhists declared that the jar contained a serpent, while Bhatta said it was the God Vishnu who has the great serpent, Sesha, as his bed. 'At these words of the Brahmin, the face of the king wore the look of the lotus that has faded in consequence of the pond wherein it grows becoming dry.' From this awkward predicament, however, the king was soon relieved, for a voice from heaven declared that the Brahmin was right and that the other party was wrong! The king thus got rid of all his doubts at once and issued this memorable edict—"Let all those of my subjects be slain who fail to slay the Buddhists, old and young, from the Himalaya mountains to the Bridge of Rama!"

It has been thought desirable to give this account of Kumarila at some length, because, among other reasons, it gives, in however distorted a form, some of the methods adopted by religious controversialists and revivalists in those days. If Bhatta really had achieved a dialectical victory at this court, as at other courts of kings and royal personages, tradition would surely have recorded it after the beaten manner. From what we have reproduced from the account given by Madhava, it seems clear that Bhatta's dialectic skill did not prove quite so successful here as it might have done elsewhere; while the test of falling down 'from the hill' or from other height was one that Kumarila had already undergone; and as to how his apparent failure to successfully guess the contents of the jar was retrieved by the support of a voice from heaven, we really cannot explain it.

With regard to the king's edict to massacre the Buddhists from the Himalaya mountains to Rama's Bridge, however, it is safe to say at once that it is mere poetic bombast, for the simple reason that previous to the days of the Mahomedan Emperors, India knew no sovereign whose sway was quite so extensive. Moreover, this same Sudhanvan who could issue such a summary edict for the destruction of Buddhists over the whole of India, is represented in another connection as hardly able to overcome a mob of Kapalika fanatics! In the declining days of Buddhism in India, the followers of that religion must in many places have been subjected to much inconvenience and even ignominy. The patronage of sovereigns and ruling chiefs, which in the earlier days had helped on the propagation of Buddhism in the country of its birth, gradually transferred its support to Hinduism so as to effect a complete reconversion of the people to a more or less new adaptation of their ancient faith. This much may be freely admitted. But to prove that there was any general persecution or massacre of the Buddhists in India, there is next to nothing in the way of adequate evidence.

For, if we content ourselves with the more or less legendary accounts of the persecution either of Buddhists in Hindustan and the

Dakhan or of Jains in Southern India, we shall have to admit that million upon millions of men were tortured or burnt or destroyed in the various diabolical ways known only to religious persecutors. But taking a more sober view of India and its people, and interpreting these legends in the light of comparison with past and present facts and of calm criticism, we have ample reason to believe that religious and political fires of persecution hardly ever discoloured the serene skies of the Indian village communities or any of those parts of the country which lay far removed from towns and cities. And even in cites the Buddhists, Jains and Hindus had, as a rule, got on well together for centuries; for, the account we have from Hiouen Tsang of the relations between the various hostile religious sects does not forebode any such coming storm as, we are asked to believe, raged over Hindustan so fiercely, under the guiding hand of Bhatta, in the very next century. Testimony from unexpected quarters continues to come in our own days to prove that a wide, fierce and relentless persecution for the sake of religion could never have been a fact in the History of India; and that those relatively few cases of persecution, which undoubtedly must have occurred at times, were confined, as a rule, to particular localities, the great capital cities usually, and probably to the 'tallest blades of the field,' *i. e.*, to the most obstinate of sectaries.

4. Bhatta and Sankara.

On the whole, however, Bhatta seems to have succeeded in converting many large provinces from Buddhism to Vedic Hinduism; and tradition confirms the fact of his having had a large following. And when he was satisfied that this work was fairly over, he is said to have resolved on the extraordinary course of committing himself to flames, of which, as has been already mentioned, news reached Sankara at Prayag, or as Chidvilasa has it, at Ruddha or Rudrapur, of which Bhadra Sena was the ruler at that time. Sankara hastened to the spot, and found Bhatta with piles of straw and dried sticks thrown about his person, all of which were already aflame. He even then caused himself to be announced to Bhatta and asked for an explanation of his course of conduct. The latter answered that on reviewing his life he had found two unpardonable sins which he had been driven to commit to further his mission. The one was the destruction of his *Guru*, Buddhist though he was, in the flame of persecution which he (Bhatta) had kindled; the other the practical denial of God in his endeavour to prove the absolute revelational character of the *Vedas* and the sole efficacy of the Vedic rites to save men. The *Smritis* having ordained self-immolation in such cases as the only proper means of purifying oneself, he had resolved on setting the example of obedience, so that the world might not have cause to say that he was a parson that recked not his own rede. Sankara, it is said, expressed a desire to have the pleasure of a discussion with him, but, as Bhatta had already become half-burnt, he could not collect his thoughts. He, therefore, asked Sankara to go to Mandana Misra, a champion of the

Karma Marga almost as good as Bhatta himself. Mandana had married Bhatta's sister and at this time was living at Mahishmati, the capital at one time of Magadha. Bhatta, after taking leave of all, passed away, leaving in the minds of many people the memory of the work for which he had lived and died.

Tragic and full of instruction his narrative undoubtedly sounds; but for purposes of history, it is to be feared that the part of the story relating to the meeting of Sankara and Bhatta is valueless; for chronology does not favour it, if we have it upon the right time for Sankara. This touching story then must be regarded, like many other touching stories, as having other uses than the historical. This remark, however, applies only to the *meeting* of the *Gurus.* It is, in all likelihood, a fact that Bhatta ended himself in that extraordinary way, for his nature, so far as tradition unfolds it, seems to have been highly emotional; and being terribly in earnest, if he had been conscious of having sinned, and conscious also that nothing short of that final step would meet the needs of the case, he obviously was not the person to shrink from that ordeal. Besides it was perfectly in keeping with the Levitical and casuistic nature of the central doctrine he had been preaching all his life.

CHAPTER IV.

THE MISSION ACCOMPLISHED.

1. Mandana Misra.

We now come to what apparently was the greatest achievement of Sankara—the controversy he had with Mandana Misra and its results. The elaboration of this event in almost all our authorities is evidence of its great importance, but strangely enough we have not many facts given about it in a plain and acceptable manner. Leaving Prayag, says Madhava, Sankara went to Mahishmati, where Mandana was living as chief Pandit of the court and in great affluence. A fine palatial house, a number of men-servants and women-servants, rows of parrots and other birds repeating the dogmatic formula of their master,—'स्वतः प्रमाणं परतः प्रमाणम्'—these are enough to show how he was living. Madhava's account places the incident of this controversy relatively at the beginning of Sankara's tour. Anandagiri, on the other hand, makes Sankara go from Rudrapur, after Bhatta's self-immolation, "northwards and reach Vidyalaya, lying to the south-east of Hastinapura, and called at that time by the people there as *Vijil Bindu*," for there lived Mandana then.

Accordingly Sankara went to Mandana's residence and met him in controversy there. What occurred at the meeting is described by Madhava, but here his authority seems to be decidedly untrustworthy. The only inference from this description seems to be that Mandana, brought up in the *Karma-mimamsa* faith, had come to entertain a constitutional hatred for *Sanyasins* (who have to give up their daily and other prescribed rites) as a class of people who were unclean and unfit for association. And we are told that he was performing a *Sraddha* ceremony, when Sankara is said to have somewhat 'dropped down' in their midst. This 'dropping down' of Sankara we shall examine presently. At once Mandana was wroth and a delectable talk ensued between the two, of which the following is a sample :— " Whence art thou shaven (one)? " " From neck upwards." "I asked the way by which thou hast managed to come." " And what did the way answer thee ? " " It answered thy mother is a widow." " Just so ; *thy* mother is, therefore, a widow, eh ? " And so on it went, growing from bad to worse, till the Brahmins who were present there for dinner interposed and pacified both !

After this fine introduction, however, Sankara desired Mandana to let him have the honour of a controversy with him. And he agreeing most readily, they sought for an empire.

2. BHARATI.

Now it so happened that Mandana had a wife of the name of Bharati, whose learning and accomplishments were very vast and many-sided, and whom accordingly they agreed to honor by appointing as an umpire. Each began with the stipulation that, in case he was defeated, he would take on himself the rule of life adopted by his opponent. In other words, Sankara, if defeated, agreed to marry and become a householder—the worst sin which a *Sanyasin* could commit. And Mandana, in a similar manner, agreed to become a *Sanyasin* and receive the red-robe from the hands of his own wife. And then the controversy continued long, day after day, without any interruption.

Bharati, according to Madhava, did not sit and listen, but was minding her household duties. At the outset she had thrown two garlands, one over the shoulders of each of the disputants, with a declaration that he whose garland should begin to fade first should consider himself defeated. After several days, Mandana's garland began to fade first. Accordingly he owned defeat, though in a sullen mood; while his wife, now that her husband was dead to her, prepared to leave home, though we are not told whither to go. In all our authorities this lady is treated as an *avatar* of the Goddess of Learning who had come down into the world by way of undergoing punishment for a piece of silliness in her heavenly abode. She laughed, it is said, at the mistake which the sage Durvasa had commited while chanting the *Vedas* before Brahma and his wife in a large assembly. The sage became enraged at the woman who had so dared to expose him to ridicule; and he pronounced this curse of earthly degradation upon her, and subsequently, after her prayers had softened his heart, he limited the period of her exile! Accordingly her period of banishment being now over, she desired to go back to her heavenly abode. It was her mission to proclaim the omniscience of Sankara to the world and having done it by means of her umpireship she was free to depart. But Sankara stopped her from going and begged the honor of having a dialectic controversy with her also; he further solicited the favour of her departing only when *he* should agree to it. Both these requests were granted to him. He now turned to Mandana still brooding over his defeat, and begged him to reconcile himself to the inevitable, seeing that Jaimini himself, the reputed author of the *Karma-Sutra*, would have agreed to his victorious interpretation of the *Sutras*. Mandana thereupon cheerfully acquiesced in his defeat, and offered to become a *Sanyasin* and follow him. But, it is strangely added, Bharati now interposed and begged the favour of a controversy with herself; for Sankara had as yet defeated but one-half of Mandana, herself being the other half! He objected to arguing with women, but she quoted precedent. So, as before, the disputation went on for seventeen days. Bharati trying to discomfit Sankara, passed from one *Sastra* to another; and finding at last that she could not inflict a defeat on him in any other science, she resolved to humble him by means of the Science of Love or *Kama-sastra*.

3. Sankara's yogic Adventures.

Now Sankara had not had the experience needed to answer questions on this science, and so found that his reputation as well as the consequent victory of his cause was at stake. So he begged of her an interval of one month for preparation to meet her in argument, which being allowed, he went to the banks of the

Narmada ; and in the hole of a tree in some forest there, he left his body in hiding, and asked some of his disciples to keep watch over it while the living soul was away from it. Then by means of his *yogic* powers he separated his soul from that body and luckily came upon the dead body of a King Amaruka, which was about to be committed to flames, and entered it. The king rose and all the town rejoiced.

However, in a short while, the ministers as well as the queens of the late king found something extraordinary about their restored sovereign, and suspected that the soul of some *Mahatman* had come to live in the body of their master. So messengers were secretly sent to search for a human body hidden in lonely forests or caves, and to burn it when found, so that the *Mahatman* might remain with them and the king continue to live for a long time. Meanwhile, Sankara in the body of the king was acquiring the experiences of love with his queens and was recording those experiences in a treatise which has come down to us under the name of *Amaruka-*

sataka. And in the midst of these lovely women and their blandishments, he forgot his promise to his disciples about his going back to them; and the month agreed upon soon passed away. The disciples then began to search for him; and hearing the miraculous resurrection of Amaruka, they went to his city, sought audience with the king, and sang a few philosophic songs which at once roused the memory of Sankara. Then they hastened to the place where the body had been secreted. But by this time the messengers of the king had found it out and had just begun to set fire to it! The unattached soul of Sankara now hastened back and entered his own body in this perilous condition. He then prayed to Vishnu conceived as Nrisimha to help him, which He did by sending down a timely shower of rain that put out the flames. Sankara was now in his own body again.

After these adventures he returned to Mandana's abode, and resuming the old controversy, satisfied Bharati on all the points raised by her, and established that he was, indeed, omniscient. Thereafter, according to Madhava, she departed back to her heavenly home. But according to Chidvilasa and others, she was still held spell-bound in the air and was taken along with Sankara to Sringeri, where he caused a temple to be built, which he dedicated to her. Here she was persuaded to take up her residence, and Bharati is even to-day worshipped by many devotees at Sringeri. And Mandana offered all his possessions as a gift to Sankara, who, however, asked him to distribute them to the poor and the deserving and then follow him, which he did. He then became a disciple of Sankara; and when he shewed himself worthy of the new philosophy of life, he was made into a *Sunyasin* with the name of Sureswara Acharya, the name by which he is known in these parts even to this day.

4. The Conversion of Mandana Restated— The Real Bharati.

This rather long and tedious account of Mandana's conversion has been given in order that we may now examine it so as to find out what exactly it was that occurred; for there certainly must be some truth at the bottom of this strange story which has been here summarised. At first sight it seems so full of incredible details and distortions that one is tempted to reject the whole of it as a tissue of fictitious fancifulness. But on a careful analysis, however, we find that two main points deserve to be noted and examined. These are (1) the incidents relating to the great lady known as Bharati, and (2) the *yogic* adventures of Sankara.

With regard to Bharati, tradition is unanimous that she was really a gifted lady, well versed in the *Sastras* and a fitting companion to the famous Pandit Mandana Misra. The theory of her being an *avatar* of the Goddess of Learning is evidently an invention of a later generation intended to honour her memory and scholarship.

Let us try to realise to ourselves the circumstances of the case. Bharati belonged to an age when learning among women was more common, and they enjoyed greater freedom, than during the centuries following the establishment of Mahomedan rule in India. For, it was one of the greatest revolutions of Buddhism to educate women for the profession of religion and make them go forth as nuns and peripatetic preachers even to distant lands. The reader will easily recollect the case of Sangamitta who thus went to Ceylon. And this spirit of Buddhism, living as it did for centuries in close contact with Hinduism, must have communicated much learning and enlightenment to Indian women of all ranks and stations in life. So that by the ninth century learning among Hindu women, especially those of high social standing, must have been a fairly common phenomenon. Bharati was, therefore, a learned lady of exceptional abilities. This fact seems to have escaped the notice of the inventors of the legend we are examining, probably because they were living in days when the dark purdah had already shut in the liberty and learning of women in India.

Accordingly, after a careful examination of the story as given by Madhava and Chidvilasa, the simple facts of the controversy and conversion may be given thus:—The disputation between the two great men was perhaps held in the presence of the king of the place. Mandana apparently set out with the rash vow of becoming *Sanyasin* in case of defeat—not a very improbable supposition in the case of one who had come to regard himself well-nigh invincible, and who had also had an irascible temper. According to his accepted doctrines, turning out a *Sanyasin* and giving up the ritualistic religion of the *Vedas*, is about the worst sin that one can commit in the world. Bharati naturally came to know of her husband's defeat and its results to her and then adopted the only sensible course that was open to a woman of her learning and character. She also renounced the world and became, as it were, a nun, and was content to accompany her converted husband wherever he went. Buddhistic nuns had been well enough known for long then. And when later on the Sringeri Mutt was established and Mandana was placed at its head as the successor of Sankara, she must have settled down there and passed her days in prayerful devotion and religious realisation, as it befitted a woman of her history and character. She was perfectly justified in the course she adopted, for though, with the donning of the red robe, Mandana had become dead to her as husband, she was, indeed, very wise in following him and Sankara in the capacity of a devoted disciple. Lastly her noble and resigned life in her later days and her peaceful end at Sringeri added lustre to her reputation for uncommon learning and wise accomplishments, and formed the groundwork of the admiration, which may even now be observed in a concrete form in the temple that has been so worthily dedicated to her at Sringeri. Indeed, there cannot be much doubt that Sankara's revival of Vedantic Hinduism in India is largely indebted to this famous and venerable lady, although we cannot now measure accurately the value of her contribution to the cause of progressive Hinduism in her days. To place her on the pedestal of immortal glory, it is enough for us to know that Sankara considered her to be worthy of worship and reverential commemoration.

5. The Yogic Miracle Examined.

If we are prepared to admit that this view is the most probable one in regard to Bharati, then the *yogic* adventures of Sankara have to be similarly examined. The possibility of one man's soul entering at his own pleasure the body of another man is not granted by modern science. The question of the reality of the soul itself is one on which modern psychology has not as yet said the last word, though the experimental psychology of the Indian *Yoga* seems, nevertheless, to be rational enough in leading us to the proof of the reality of the soul. But all those wonder-working *Yogic* powers, which are amply described in Hindu, Jain, and Buddhistic writings, are things about which the best attitude now is one of suspended judgment. Accordingly the whole story of the transference of Sankara's soul into Amaruka's body has to be rejected as being undemonstrable, the more because the motive assigned for this adventure is after all very silly and inconsistent with the learning and subsequent conduct of Bharati. In so treating this question of soul-transference, however, it is not meant to condemn the philosophy or the psychology or the practice of *Yoga* as being in itself impossible —that will be going out of the way and highly presumptuous. But with all the difference due to those who believe in *yoga*, however, we may say that the works of the Teacher, which luckily we still possess, are miraculous enough to satisfy the most exacting expectations of the most ardent admirer. We shall accordingly venture to conclude that the whole of this episode is due to the misguided enthusiasm of later admirers, from whom every great person has reason to pray to be saved.

The result of Sankara's advent to Mahishmati was not merely that Mandana was converted, but that the king and his court were likewise converted so as to follow his doctrines. For Sankara, while emphasising *jnana* or knowledge of the Supreme Spirit as the chief object of man's endeavours, here on earth, did not go the length of rejecting all the other means of attaining the *summum bonum*, as Bhatta and other controversialists had egotistically done before. This spirit of compromise, in all likelihood, made his work easier; for there was but little revolutionary in his contentions. The lovers of ceremonialism were allowed to go on with their *Karmas*—only the spirit which underlay the doing of them had to become different.

6. Tour through the Dakhan Districts.

Having done his work at Mahishmati, Sankara left with his disciples for the South of India and passed through Maharashtra preaching his doctrines wherever he went. He denounced all wicked practices, and sent forth disciples, where he could not go himself, to spread the light of the Vedanta. A class of Brahmins here worshipped Siva under the name of Mallari, and religiously honoured and exalted the position of the dog, which was the animal that this God loved to ride on. Vedic text such as श्वभ्यः श्वपतिभ्यश्च वोनमोनमः । were quoted to support it. But Sankara could easily prove that they were hopelessly in the wrong, and show them that the dog, being an unclean animal, did not deserve any worship. Mallari is even now known to be the tutelary deity of many Mahratta families, and at the festival of Dasara that deity receives special worship at their hands. But his dog or dogs are not heard of in our days as objects of worship.

There was likewise the sect of *Kapalikas* of atrocious memory whom Sankara encountered hereabout. From one of them he seems to have had a narrow escape. The favourite deity of the *Kapalikas* is Bhairava, the Destroyer, who has a peculiar fondness for the heads of learned Brahmins; the more learned and pious, the better ! Such a head presented to him streaming with warm blood had been conceived to be the most acceptable offering. A section of Mahratta Brahmins of the name of *Karadis* have had a bad reputation among the people of South India for catching stray pilgrims from the South to Benares and, after fattening them for a whole year, offering them to Durga in sacrifice at the close of the Dasara as an acceptable and a highly valuable offering. This charge against them is nothing new, and it was in all likelihood a *Karadi* Brahmin of these parts that approached Sankara at this time with the object of sacrificing him to Kali. There is nothing unique about this belief in human sacrifice, for history has known it all the world over in very many repulsive and piteous forms.

Madhava says that the *Kapalika* approached Sankara and begged for his head as a gift, employing certain sophistries of *Advaitism* to prove that Sankara could not lose anything by the loss of the head, while he himself gained thereby the highest object of his attainment. Sankara agreed and asked him to come and take it, while he was alone and was absorbed in contemplation. Accordingly the *Kapalika* went and was just aiming the fatal blow, when Padmapada, who had just then returned, caught hold of his uplifted arm, knocked him down and killed him with his own weapon. Madhava in relating this killing of the *Kapalika* says that the spirit of the fierce God Narasimha was then on Padmapada, and that Sankara finding out what had taken place managed to pacify the infuriated disciple.

7. THE SRINGERI MUTT.

Then he travelled to the south till he reached the source of the Tungabhadra, where he stopped and built a temple, which he dedicated to the Goddess of Learning. Under the name of Sarada, that Goddess is to this day the presiding deity of the temple there. Chidvilasa says that he was helped in this work by a local chief of the name of Vira-Sena. To the temple he attached a *Mutt* and placed the most learned of his disciples, Mandana, at its head, with the name of Sureswara Acharya, by which name he is still known in the records of that Mutt. The institution is "the Sringeri Mutt" of to-day, the most richly endowed and the most widely honoured of South Indian Religious Institutions.

Madhava here gives an account of the daily monastic life of Sankara, which is just what one finds in Mutts even in our own days—with the exception that there was then much original teaching and composition going on therein, because of the presence of the Founder of a new School of Philosophy.

8. THE GLOSS OF PADMAPADA.

In connection with the work of religious and philosophic teaching here at Sringeri, we come upon an exhibition of jealousy among the disciples. Even in matters which the *Guru* might view as peculiarly his own, he did not always find it possible to have his own way. At this time Sankara was desirous that his commentary on the *Vedanta-Sutras* should have a gloss added to it to prevent misconception and to supply ellipses. He seems to have felt convinced that Mandana's learning both in the *Karmic* and in his own philosophy, had fitted him best for his task, and he, therefore, asked him to carry it out. At once Sankara's other disciples set up Padmapada, the earliest and undoubtedly the most devoted of his followers, to do the same work. They argued plausibly enough that Mandana's conversion was on account of his defeat in controversy, and was not, therefore, the result of hearty conviction.

They feared that his gloss might prove dangerous to Sankara's system, for he might unconsciously or even deliberately show leanings towards the faith in which he had been brought up before. They, therefore, thought that Padmapada should be asked to do it, for his devotion to the *Guru* had been well tested and he had all the teachings of the *Guru* imparted to him-thrice over by the *Guru* himself. Although he was born a *Prabhakara*, he had been well enough weaned from his earlier faith even in his youth; and had, therefore, as they contended, become worthy of the honor and trust implied in the permission granted to annotate the *Guru's* works. Padmapada, however, suggested Anandagiri or Hastamalaka, who had joined Sankara in his tour through Maharashtra, in order that he himself might appear less selfish in the eyes of his teacher. Sankara felt perplexed and vexed. He felt sure that Mandana was, by his intimate knowledge of the strong and weak points of the *Karma-mimamsa* philosophy, the best fitted among his disciples; yet 'in this great undertaking, he did not want to go against the wishes of the majority among them.' So he suffered Padmapada to do the work in spite of his own misgivings, and was really sorry that his great commentary had to lose the benefit of the gloss of so valuable a scholar as Mandana. To console the latter, however, Sankara allowed him to annotate his commentaries on the chief *Upanishads* and also to compose one or two original works. This unseemly quarrel shows the spirit of the age and the suspicion which ever haunts the faithful in full proportion to the intensity of their faith. It seems to be the curse from which the followers of no great religious teacher can be said to have been free. The reader of the Bible will easily recollect the quarrel among the disciples of Christ for precedence.

Padmapada then annotated his master's commentary on the *Vedanta-Sutras*, and in doing it he exposed the flaws of the *Prabhakara* school of the *Purva-mimamsa* to ridicule over and over again. He seems to have been 'a vain man'; for, having done this work, he asked the *Guru's* permission to go to Rameswar—perhaps to parade his learning in the land of his birth. Permission having been given, he went to Chidambaram (his 'native place' according to Chidvilasa), which was at that time the stronghold of the *Prabhakara* faith. Here Padmapada stayed with his uncle, who was still a follower of the *Prabhakara* faith. This person happening to read portions of his nephew's gloss on Sankara's great commentary, resolved to wreak his vengeance on the manuscript ! And Padmapada, having in a moment of weakness agreed to leave his books behind him, and set out for Rameswar, in his absence the uncle contrived to consign the books to the flame. On the nephew's return, he, of course, expressed great sorrow for the mishap. Padmapada was at a loss to know how then to proceed and was not sure if he could do the work again so well. It is added that his uncle had also had the villainy to drug him with a view to spoil his intelligence. He at last returned with a drooping heart and joined his master once again.

CHAPTER V.

LAST DAYS.

1. SANKARA'S MOTHER—HER FUNERAL RITES.

And now we come to the most pathetic part of Sankara's life. Tradition is unanimous herein, and there is nothing in the narrative to make it in itself improbable. Some time after Padmapada left for Rameswar, Sankara, either longing to see his mother or having had news conveyed to him of the declining state of her health, left his disciples behind at Sringeri, and went apparently all alone to Kaladi. His mother was then bed-ridden, and was, of course, exceedingly glad to see him. He touched her feet in reverence—setting the rules of *Sanyasa* at defiance. Being very ill and her thoughts all turned to the other world, she desired her son, whose fame had doubtless reached her ears, to discourse to her on things that would bestow peace and salvation on her soul. He began to preach to her his high philosophy, evidently underrating the difficulties in comprehending it. So the mother desired him to tell her of things which she could easily understand. Accordingly he glorified Siva in a hymn of praise composed by himself. The messengers of Siva soon made their appearance, but their terrific shapes were too much for her and she refused to go along with them to the world of Siva. Then Sankara praised Vishnu; and his messengers coming down in bright and agreeable forms, she blessed her son, gave up her body and went along with them to the abode of Vishnu.

The mother being dead, Sankara sought to fulfil the promise he had made to her at the time of his renunciation, and desired to perform her funeral rites himself. This, however, was not easy, for the whole *Agrahara* opposed it as being against the *Smritis* and established practice; and Nambudris, of all the orthodox people in the world, are the last to suffer any deviation from the clerical law to occur in their midst unopposed. If Sankara was a *Sanyasin*, as he said he was, he had nothing to do with funeral rites; and if he persisted in performing them, he was clearly an impostor in the garb of a *Sanyasin*, and must be hunted like a heretic and sinner. Arguing the affair in this manner, the relatives of Sankara held aloof and in spite of his entreaties they would neither help him to remove the dead body, nor, as tradition pathetically adds, let him have fire to burn it with. Unable to soften their hearts, he resolved to do the rites without anybody's help; and girding himself up for it, he bore the body of his mother to the back-yard of the house, and making there a pyre with dried sticks he laid the body on it, *made* fire for the cremation and performed all the rites pertaining to the funeral ceremony. Tradition further adds that, unable to remove the body entire, he cut it and removed the pieces one by one—and, having found only stems of the plantain tree for fuel, he exercised his divine power and set them on fire!

2. REMARKS THEREON.

The funeral rites being over, he sought to find some means of revenging himself on his heartless relatives. Madhava adds an apology for this fit of anger, and says—'Although some of the deeds of the great do not seem to conform to *Shastraic* rules ordinarily observed, such persons are not to be censured on that account.' Sankara is said to have persuaded the local chief to issue an edict prohibiting those relatives from chanting the *Vedas* and thus making them unfit to entertain *Sanyasins* as guests. They were further compelled to set apart in each *Illam* a corner of its own compound to burn the dead of the family, and to see that every dead body should be cut into parts and then burnt!

Now it cannot be denied that Hindu Princes have often issued edicts, changing religious and social practices or the status of particular classes among their subjects. There are many historic instances to illustrate this. Indeed, there would have been nothing strange in what this local chief is alleged to have done at the instigation of Sankara, if we can be sure that he, in fact, had had sufficient influence for it at the court of this local chieftain. But, beyond the bare mention of a 'Rajasekhara' referred to just before the *Guru's* renunciation, who on one occasion at that period is said to have gone to the young Brahmin to have a view of one whose great learning had already begun to be noised abroad, Madhava tells us little from which Sankara's influence at his court may well be estimated. Accordingly the whole question of this supposed edict looks suspicious for want of conclusive evidence. It is a fact, however, which may interest many readers, that the Nambudris continue to this day the formality of mangling the dead bodies of their relations before they are removed to the place of cremation. A knife is made just to touch the various joints of the body. It is also a fact in most, if not all, the *Illams* of the Nambudris that a corner of their spacious compound serves as the cremation ground of the family. And, lastly, it is a fact also that some among the Nambudris do not learn how to chant the

Vedas. If called on to explain the origin of any of these practices, they repeat the story of the edict and say that the observances have continued so long as to become included in *their Smritis.*

The tale relating to the funeral rites makes just one thing clear that Sankara failed to become a prophet in his own land. There is but one difficulty, however, in the way of our admitting the whole of this story as true. For, if Sankara's name and fame had spread so far and so wide, as we may naturally infer from the story of his tour and his controversies as recorded, it certainly looks very odd that, during the whole of this troublous period of his mother's funeral ceremonies, there was not a single disciple by him to help him. This difficulty Madhava avoids by representing that Sankara had left every one of his disciples behind, and hastened to his mother's home on learning that she was seriously ill. Perhaps Anandagiri is right in placing the incident of the death of Sankara's mother at an earlier period in his life.

Viewed as a whole, the narrative relating to the funeral rites of Sankara's mother is exceedingly instructive as an act of rare filial affection, furnishing to common men one of the best illustrations of the moral beauty and sublimity which are to be found in the noble duty of a man having to honour the sacred memory of his mother.

3. Tour through the East Coast Districts.

Returning to Sringeri, he set out some time afterwards with a large number of followers on a tour through the eastern coast, stopping in important centres of learning, at the capitals of kings and places of pilgrimage, to preach his doctrines and to condemn whatever wicked practices were therein prevalent. At Puri he established a *Mutt* which still goes by the name of *Govardhan Mutt.* Conjeeveram seems at that time to have been a stronghold of *Saktas,* whom Sankara is said to have argued out of their abominations. He purified their temples; and the pre-eminence, which the Goddess Kamaktshi of Kanchi and Minakshi of Madura have to this day preserved, would seem to bear out the prevalence at one time of Sakti-worship in all these regions and its purification under Brahminical influence. But it is perhaps dangerous to theorise too much. We are briefly told that in the course of this tour the kings of the Chola and Pandya kingdoms were won over. The net result of the tour was that the abominations of the *Saktas*, *Ganapathyas*, *Kapalikas* and the rest of their tribe received a severe check ; and permanent arrangements were made at Sringeri to periodically attack the centres of immoral and unholy religious rites so as to chase them away altogether in due course. This tour of reformation and religious purification must have lasted fairly long.

4. Final Tour through Hindustan.

At length, after making arrangements to carry on his missionary work in the south and after firmly establishing the Sringeri Mutt with a proper staff, Sankara left once again for the north. Passing through the Berars he stopped for some time at Ujjain. From the *Meghadûta* of Kalidasa, as well as from other sources, we learn that some kind of *Saiva* worship was prevalent here, which apparently needed the shedding of a good deal of the blood of sacrificial victims. Madhava calls the devotees of this deity by the name of Bhairavas; and with this sect Sankara began to argue and denounce their iniquities, which roused the mob there, whose leader was significantly called Krakacha, which means a saw. Madhava brings in here once again King Sudhanvan who has already been mentioned. The fact seems to be that Sankara first won over the local chief to his faith, and with his help put down the atrocities of the Bhairavas by force, when perhaps argument had proved to be of no avail with them. Thence he passed on to Guzarat and there at Dwaraka established a Mutt which is in existence even now and has some following. He then travelled along the course of the Ganges, in which journey he is said to have won victories in controversy over many great personages such as Bhaskara, Bana, Dandin, Mayura and others. But if the date we have accepted is the correct one for Sankara, many of these controversial victories have to be treated as inventions. He is also said to have gone to Kashmir to win the famous Seat of Learning there, which was meant as a prize to the wisest of men; and this information is useful perhaps as showing that Buddhists could be found in large numbers chiefly in the Himalayan regions even in Sankara's days.

5. Abhinava Gupta—Sankara's End.

The last controversial victory, which seems to have much to support its reality, was at Kamrup, or Gauhati, as it is now called, in Assam, where Sankara triumphed over the *Sakta* commentator Abhinava Gupta. This man felt his defeat so keenly that he resolved to be somehow revenged on his opponent. Accordingly he utilised his knowledge of Black Magic, and by means of it caused Sankara to be afflicted with a very serious form of hemorrhoids; and though he did not mind it for a while, the disciples who were doing him personal service soon saw that the disease was growing upon him; and they are said to have consulted many doctors and tried many prescriptions in vain. At length a messenger from Siva came and revealed the secret. At once Padmapada was wroth, and being a clever hand himself in the Black Art, he undid Gupta's evil work very easily and Sankara became whole as before.

Although we are told that Sankara thus got well, what followed soon after shows that the disease must have severely told on him, and that there was only some temporary relief, during which he managed to go to Badari and establish a Mutt there as well as build a temple to Narayana. After this he retired to Kedarnath. And here, in his thirty-second year, as it is stated by Madhava and several others, or in his thirty-eighth year, as another tradition has it (which latter is accepted by the present writer), the great Teacher passed away in the year A. D. 828.

CHAPTER VI.

THE WORK OF SANKARA.

1. The Mutts.

It is not proposed in this sketch to trace the fortunes of Sankara's system in times later than his own, or those of his successors at the various Mutts established by him. In the first place, the materials are not available for it; and in the next such a description is outside our limits. It is enough for our purpose to say that the four Mutts we have incidentally mentioned continue to exist in greater or less affluence even now, after having had their usual ups and downs in the course of about twelve historic centuries. The *Sringeri Mutt*, in our own parts, knew very bright days during the beginning and early development of the Vijianagar Kingdom, but it is to be feared that even this Mutt has got but few valuable records to enable one to write its history.

These Mutts, though founded by the same Teacher and for the same purpose, have had but little connection with each other, administrative, social or religious. But, at the same time, there has been no rivalry known between any two of them, India having apparently proved wide enough for all of them to work smoothly on. There has been, however, one small secession in the south caused by the establishment of a Mutt now at Kumbakonam, which has a limited following in Tanjore and the adjoining districts. That this Kumbakonam Mutt is comparatively modern, appears to be probable, though its exact age cannot be well ascertained.

2. THE CARDINAL DOCTRINE OF SANKARA AND ITS GENESIS.

It is now our business to examine the net result of Sankara's life and labours. We have already taken note of what the tune was that was haunting millions of ears about his time. We saw how Buddhism rose from the *Upanishads*, grew, and after a long life decayed in the land of its birth. It is often said that Buddhism disappeared from India by persecution. We have ample testimony, however, to prove that this persecution is a myth. Buddhism simply lost itself in the revived Hinduism. A long course of peaceful life side by side had certainly led to many silent assimilations and natural borrowings—the practical abolition of animal sacrifices, the gorgeous and elaborate festivals and processions, and the owning of Buddha as an *avatar* of Vishnu, being some of those that lie on the surface. On the side of thought this process culminated in the practical acceptance and wide adoption of the *Bhagavad-Gita* and its most comprehensive philosophy, which, unlike the old 'exclusive' religion of the *Vedas*, may be followed and practised by all classes of people. Furthermore, the most prominent failings of Buddhism came to be noted and guarded against to save Hinduism from a like fate. For instance, the *Bhakti-Marga* or the path of love and devotion to God, as explained in some of the most eloquent passages of the

Bhagavata or *Vishnu-Purana*, is an open protest against the atheism of Buddhists. Again, while orders of monks were being slowly organised in imitation of Buddhists, care was taken to rigorously exclude women from them.

Having been born and brought up amidst such circumstances, Sankara soon carved out for himself at a very early stage of his life a clear and definite course. It was to give a common basis to the most prevalent forms of the Vedic faith and to reconcile all these to a cardinal co-ordinating idea. Hence arose his Pantheism, which sees the Great First Cause, the Essence of Intelligence, everywhere about us and in us. With the help of this doctrine, supported as it is by many Vedic texts, it was easy for his master-mind to show, wherever he went, that the current religious sects were all narrow and illogical, and, that if properly understood, there was no real antagonism at all between the rival sects and no good ground for the rise of bad blood in the practice of religion or the contemplation of philosophy.

3. The End and the Means.

For our immediate purpose, we must be satisfied with a bare statement of his chief doctrines. He started with the hypothesis of a *Maya* or *Avidya*, an Ignorance which is objective.* Nothing really exists but the Supreme Spirit, so that what is commonly called Nature (animate and inanimate) is but an illusion and a dream, caused by this Ignorance which surrounds the Supreme Spirit, and hides It, "even as the smoke that rises from the fire hides the blaze for a time." Phenomena appear real, for the same reason that things seen in a dream are real so long as the dream lasts, or for the reason that mother-of-pearl is mistaken for silver, or a piece of rope for a snake, until the illusion goes away. The business of life is, therefore, to cast off the gross sheaths that surround the spirit within us, and to *realise* its identity with the Supreme Spirit. The chief means of attaining this end is the cultivation of true

* एवमयमनादिरनन्तो नैसर्गिकोऽध्यासो मिथ्याप्रत्ययरूप : सर्वलोकप्रत्यक्ष : । *Sutra-Bhashya.*

knowledge, that is, the study of the *Vedanta* and the incessant contemplation of its teachings. Special emphasis had to be laid on this means, as Sankara had found that Bhatta had 'bent the bow too much on the other side' and held that the purely physical *Karma* or going through a round of ritualistic formalities was alone sufficient to secure salvation. In all doctrinal passages, therefore, he gives prominence to the acquisition of Vedantic knowledge. But that does not mean, however, that he rejected the other means, for he accepted the *Karmic* road also as one of the roads to take the soul finally to the goal. Again, nowhere in his writings is he more eloquent than in his songs in exemplification and praise of the *Bhakti-Marga.*

The Supreme Spirit of Sankara is free from all real attributes, and the only positive statement that can be made about it is that It is and is the Essence of Intelligence and Bliss. This has led the author of *Manimanjari* to say that Sankara has called Nothingness by the name of *Brahman,* and a recent writer to declare that 'he retained the name of God to save his religion from becoming Buddhistic atheism'. Now it cannot be denied that Buddhistic philosophy had had considerable effect on him, though it is hard to measure the extent of that influence. But in every sensible statement of Sankara's teachings, one sees Pantheism and not Atheism governing them. *And Pantheism and Atheism must always be poles apart,* state it how we will.

The end of man being the realisation of the identity of his own spirit with the Supreme Spirit, and the study of Vedanta and the contemplation of its teachings being the best means of attaining it, Sankara also recommended less difficult paths of salvation for such people as are not fitted for that kind of self-realisation. The practice of self-denial and of other moral virtues, devotion to God and the careful discharge of each man's duties, as ordained by the scriptures, are declared by him to be preliminaries to acquiring in due course the needed moral competency for the study of the Vedanta and the realisation of its ideals. Man is to do his secular as well as religious duties, not because it will give him good things here or in the other world, as Bhatta had said, but because they have to be done; and at every step the *Vedantin* is called upon to bear in mind these sublime words of the *Gita* :—" The master of the sacrifice, who is Brahman, has thrown into the sacrificial fire which is Brahman, the saorificial rice which is Brahman, for the satisfaction of Brahman; and that which that master wants to attain is likewise Brahman !"

This comprehensive and pantheistic basis, while it enabled the hitherto hostile sects to worship each its own deity as before, showed at the same time conclusive reasons for mutual toleration and friendliness. Sankara's mission, looked at thus, was therefore not to destroy but to fulfil, ' for it was by no means suppression of acts of outward devotion nor of the preferential worship of any acknowledged preeminent Deity. So when the admission was made that *Brahman* was the Supreme Spirit, the First Cause as distinct from Siva or Vishnu the Teacher left undisturbed, *having regard to human frailties*, the observance of such rites and worship of such deities as are either prescribed by the Vedas or of works not incompatible with their authority.' Of these deities *five* had already become recognised as deserving worship at the hands of every Vedic sect—the *Bhagavata*, for instance, mentions it —and the worshippers of these five comprised the bulk of the people, though each sect was subdivided into a large number of mutually repellant groups. They were the Sun, Ambika (Sakti), Vishnu, Ganapati and Siva. Everywhere, at the conclusion of the controversy, the precept given was the same—offer worship to the five Gods. This was how Sankara sought to unite these enemies and to counteract their 'particularist' tendencies. It never occurred to him to talk as the advocates of some militant faiths had done before him, or have done since, to claim all wisdom for himself and locate all folly in his opponents, crediting them with nothing but folly. It is for the candid reader to judge whether the result has justified the founder's expectations, and history has since proved how far his measures have softened sectarian bigotry and the consequent rise of bad blood.

4. His Method.

As his plans were moderate and conciliatory, so was his method agreeable and perhaps about the best to be employed in such matters. Anandagiri is specially valuable in giving us a fair idea of what this method was. Wherever he went, he asked the leaders of thought who opposed him to state their case and explain their doctrines and practices. After they did it, he began to point out how far he could go with them—and in the case of most of them he could go with them some way, as they had all based their faith on the authority of the Vedas. Next came the points of difference—philosophic as well as practical. Those who quoted stray sentences (as the Mallari-worshippers did) from the Vedas in support of their objectionable doctrines or practices, he could answer by quite a host of passages quoted against them; and those who had based their evil doings on *Smritis* were told that it was a well-understood axiom that, as against *Srutis*, *Smritis* could not stand, and that as against *Smritis*, *Puranas* could not stand. One or two small instances must suffice to illustrate this method. The champions of Sun-worship argued that that luminary was Supreme Spirit, because a well-known text says—"This Sun is Brahman." But Sankara could quote a number of texts to the contrary, for instance, one which runs—"The Sun shines from fear of this (Brahman);" or again—"The Sun, the Moon...all shine with the light borrowed from this Supreme Light," and so on. The worshippers of Siva or Vishnu or Ganapati could likewise receive no support from the Vedas, and the authority of the Vedas herein was supreme; and passage after passage followed in defence of this position. No wonder that, with this kind of tact as well as argument, he was able to influence thoughtful people everywhere. How different this from the method which has been pursued by many another teacher in India, and from the one which is being commonly pursued by our *Padri* friends and people of their likeness! These latter begin wherever they go by arrogating to themselves the whole truth and nothing but the truth, leaving with a unique impartiality to their opponents, the whole of the error and nothing but error.

If any person's style is an index of his mind, the style of Sankara's is one. It has been said that 'the sublimest philosophy expresses itself in the simplest language,' and, if we want the best illustration to prove it, we have to go to Sankara for it. Bewitching and marvellous and simple, it is at once the language of the child and the philosopher in one. No wonder then that enemies should bear testimony to it, even while they malign his doctrines. Viewed from any standpoint, it is truly a privilege to read a bit of him or hear some of his *slokas* sung to you. He is, therefore, undoubtedly the great भद्रंकर, 'factor for good' to whoever cares to approach him.

5. His Chief Practical Reforms.

We might now take a rapid survey of the chief practical reforms which the Guru was able to effect either himself directly, or through the agency of his successors working on the lines sketched out by him. They are, from one point of view, of greater interest to us than his doctrines which can, at all times, be understood and utilised only by a few. It might be that Sankara did not accomplish all the reforms ascribed to him during the short period of his mission, but that he sketched the lines on which his successors worked. But it might also be that those days were more plastic than our own, because Hinduism was then living in closer contact with an aggressive offspring of its own, which had even in its early days achieved astounding success. Then again both Buddhistic and Hindu kings were freely issuing edicts introducing changes in faith and in social practice. People, therefore, in those days, and even long after Sankara's time, could have had no idea of the chill process of crystallisation that has come upon our life since, and has frozen the genial current of our soul with that withering curse of each being wise in his own conceit and each deluding himself with the belief that he lives in the best of all worlds; and being accustomed to changes, gentle as well as violent, they easily suffered their practices to change, wherever there was any need for it. At all events the thinking people had not in those days been brought up, as they too often are now, in the belief that the would had never changed and that every local practice had remained just what it was in the days of Manu!

According to our authorities, the chief reforms with which Sankara concerned himself were the following :—

(1) Prohibition of marking the body with hot metallic designs. Readers can easily understand what this means. The Sri-Vaishnavas and Madhvas continue to this day to mark every one among them on the shoulders and elsewhere with the designs of the conch and disc of Vishnu. Anandagiri makes a great deal too much of this reform, and Madhava likewise lays much stress on it. This circumstance throws some doubt on the value of these books as original authorities, and leads one to ask oneself whether, after all, some of these might not have been counterblasts to hostile books

finding favour with the public—for instance, मध्व विजय.

(2) No sects that Sankara had to contend against were found to have fallen so low in morality as the Saktas and the Bhairavas. The former in these days are happily found but in few localities, Assam being the most prominent of them, and the Coromandel Coast showing stray cases here and there. The sect is, as is well known, 'divided against itself,' and the *Samachara* or left-handed variety of it, is the most loathsome form that religion has ever assumed. The *Dakshinachara* or right-handed variety has been influenced by the superior moral atmosphere surrounding it, so as to make its once detestable practices comparatively innocent 'to suit the iron age of Kali.'* If in our own days the abominations of the Saktas have learned to hide their heads in shame, and are found only in some dark corners, no small

---

* These statements have drawn from the *Theosophist* some remarks about all of us moving in the direction of *Dakshinathara* Saktas in some occult way. But as this sketch has followed the logic of common sense throughout, it is hoped that the kind reviewer will not take it amiss that the writer still remains obdurate.

part of the credit is due to the chastening influence of Sankara's teaching and his earnest endeavour to put evil down. He also fought against the hideous worshippers of Ganapati whose ritual decency forbids us to describe. In both these cases, however, be it noted, the actual worship of Sakti and of Ganapati was retained, but the abominations connected therewith were condemned and abolished.

(3) If he used arguments against the Saktas he did not hesitate to use force, wherever he could, against the Bhairavas or Kapalikas, who in any age and under any circumstances would deserve that and even worse treatment. Although we may make large allowances in their favour, the account we have of their ways is so horrid and detestable that no one can have anything but praise to offer to Sankara for his labours against this pestilential religious sect.

6. SANKARITE MONKS.

Lastly, he organised Mutts and organised ten definite orders of *Sanyasin* under the name *Dasnamis*, probably in unconscious imitation of similar Buddhistic organisations. The continuation of the Mutts was provided for by the institution of a succession of *Sanyasin* chiefs, while their safety was entrusted to neighbouring rulers who had usually become converts to the new faith. The *Dasnamis* add at the end of their names any one of the following suffixes, *Saraswati*, *Bharati*. *Puri*, *Giri*, *Tirtha*, *Asrama*, *Vana*, *Aranya*, *Parvata* and *Sagara*. This list is seen occasionally in slightly altered forms. Some of the *Sanyasins* at the head of the Sringeri Mutt have been *Bharatis* (the present incumbent is also one), and there was at least one *Aranya* in Vidyaranya. These *Sanyasins* are recruited from all castes, and some rise to become *Ativarnasramis* (superior to caste observances), and dine with all classes of people without suffering for it in the estimation of the 'high born.' Perhaps this is due to the silent influence of the Buddhistic rules which from their very beginning had forbidden caste scruples within the monasteries. The *Paramahamsas* represent the highest of these grades, and one can attain this grade only by a long course of holy life and the gathering of Vedantic knowledge. In other words, men rise to be *Paramahamsas* by merit and Sankara's writings invariably have the following colophon :—" Thus is this finished which has been composed by Sankara Bhagavatpada, the best of peripatetic teachers of the grade of *Paramahamsas*, and the disciple of Sri Govinda Bhagavatpada."

Profiting by the lessons which the Buddhistic inclusion of women as *Parivrajikas* in the body of ordained ascetics had taught, and true to the old ideal of the *Smritis* under which women were never allowed independence, Sankara rigorously excluded women from his monasteries, which were meant to serve only as schools of learning, as peripatetic teaching institutions, and as asylums for those men who courted poverty and purity and freedom from the thraldom of the world.

7. THE RESULTS—THE FUTURE.

The effect of these doctrinal and practical reforms has had a widespread and far-reaching importance. We have often heard it said that Hinduism has been unique in that it has been able to assimilate alien faiths and include them within itself. Accordingly it has also been said that it is the most tolerant of the religions of the world. In so far as these statements are true, one of the best expounders in comparatively later times of this comprehensive and tolerant Hinduism was, by general consent, Sankara. His followers are of course heterogeneous in composition, but taken on the whole they form, according to Mr. L. Rice in the *Mysore Gazetteer*, and according to a host of other observant authorities, the most tolerant of the Hindu sects. This then is one of Sankara's chief claims on our admiration. There have, indeed, been reformers since his time, some of them working in a wider sphere like Kabir and Nanak, who sought to unite in harmony even the Hindus and the Muhammadans; but so far as toleration and breadth of view are concerned, within the pale of Hinduism itself, most subsequent movements must be called retrograde.

The one weak point in Sankara's system may now be noted as having formed the underlying cause of subsequent secessions. We saw that he was forced to lay unusual stress in *jnana* or the true realisation of God and, like Socrates of old, sought " to rationalise the whole Universe " to counteract the extravagances of Bhatta. Now this kind of wisdom is clearly not within the reach of common men, to whom Sankara's teaching is accordingly a sealed book. Then again, a little knowledge which is dangerous in all cases, is most dangerous here, and is apt to give rise to many pious humbugs and deluded weaklings who will cite Scripture for their own purposes. Further, even among the most learned in Sankara's school of Vedanta a tendency has often been seen to make religion more an affair of the head than of the heart. And notwithstanding his great eloquence in praise of *Bhakti* or religious devotion, the injunction given to the less gifted and therefore the great majority of his followers to keep mechanically repeating the formula ' I am *Brahman* ' is but a sorry substitute for genuine and intelligible *Bhakti.* This, it cannot be denied, began to be felt in succeeding times and led to the subsequent '*Bhagavata*' movements in the eleventh, twelfth, and the following centuries.

Another charge against him has been brought by those who have been most opposed to his philosophy—that he has by force read his own doctrines into the *Sutras* of Badarayana. But we have already seen that not merely Sankara, but every other philosopher or poet known to history has had to inhale much before he could exhale, so that his commentary on the *Vedanta Sutras* includes not only the meaning of the original, but also all the explanations that had been given by subsequent students before his time; and naturally his own peculiar views and doctrines are also embodied therein, for otherwise he would have *founded* nothing. There is nothing to marvel here for the student of history, for all commentators have at all times done the same thing more or less. Great men as well as little men "can never escape from the influence of the process in which they form part." And as for the *Sutras*, it is in their nature to be easily elastic; and when unsupported by tradition, nothing, indeed, can be made out of them. Accordingly this objection is no objection, for if it is admitted, every teacher suffers, while if we disregard परपरा, we cut ourselves adrift.

During the last fifty years, if not for a longer time, Sankara and his philosophy have received additional importance through the zeal of Western scholars and Theosophists, and he now has admirers in lands of which he could never have even dreamt. His philosophy is being subjected to the usual processes of comparison and criticism, wherever its study has been earnestly taken up. If it can continue to stand the tests of thought and time in future, as it has done in the past, there is certainly a bright prospect before it. If, however, at any future date, the human mind outgrows the limits of Sankara's philosophy, mankind will surely value it even then as a substantial contribution leading to the Infinite growth of knowledge of which the *Sruti* sings, वेदावाएते । अनन्तावैवेदाः । All true and noble work in the building up of progress and civilisation is of this nature, and as the tower rises higher and higher the lower levels thereof become the inevitable supports of the higher elevation; and the lower they are, the greater is the weight of the superincumbent edifice that rests on them.

THE PHILOSOPHY OF SANKARACHARYA.

I. SANKARA APPEALS TO REASON, NOT TO MERE AUTHORITY.

Leaving aside more exact definitions of philosophy, definitions which are not likely to be intelligible to the ordinary, unphilosophical reader, we may define Philosophy, for our present purpose, as a reasoned theory of the Universe, a theory that endeavours to explain the mutual relations of Nature, Man and God. Philosophy must, at the least, be such a theory, whatever else it may be. Now, do the writings of Sankaracharya really contain a philoshphy in this sense of the term ? We ask this question at the very outset, because such a question is often asked by the superficial reader of Sankara's writings, and answered in the negative. Such a reader sees that Sankara ever and anon speaks of himself as a mere expounder of the utterances of the ancient sages of India—the *rishis* of the *Upa-*

nishads, the composer of the Vedanta aphorisms, and the author of the *Bhagavad-Gita*. At almost every step he appeals to the Vedas as the ultimate authority on matters spiritual, and seems to deny that man can know God by unaided Reason. In his commentary on the sixth *anuvak* of the 'Brahmananda Valli' of the *Taittiriya Upanishad*, he distinctly says: "The *Sruti* is our source of knowledge in matters transcending the senses." A reader of the class mentioned above may, therefore, naturally conclude that Sankara's system is not a philosophy in any proper sense of the term. But a careful reader of his writings will observe, that, notwithstanding Sankara's great regard for scriptural authority, and his anxiety to show that his system is based on such authority, unlike the systems of the Sankhyas and the Nayayikas, which he characterises as unscriptural, he reasons a good deal, and defends all his leading doctrines by arguments addressed to the understanding of his readers. It is also seen that what he calls *Sruti* or Revelation is nothing spiritual insight and experience and that by setting up the Vedas as our authority on spiritual matters, he means nothing more than this, that the recorded experiences of the *rishis* turn our eyes inward and thus help us to see, with the eyes of the spirit, the Supreme Self in which all souls and all things rest. His appeal to Scripture is not as to an external authority to be blindly received, but as to a valuable help to the attainment of true wisdom—wisdom which is attainable by every qualified seeker after truth. As he says in his commentary on the *Prasnopanishad, VI.* 2—"The use of a scriptural text is not to alter existing things, but to make them appear as they are." Again, at the end of his commentary on the tenth *anuvak* of the 'Siksha Valli' of the *Taittiriya Upanishad*, he says: "Thus is it shown that the visions of the *rishis* concerning the soul and such other matters, manifest themselves to one who is devoted to the constant duties prescribed by the *Srutis* and the *Smritis*, who is unselfish and who seeks to know the Supreme Brahman." By what actual arguments Sankara establishes the different tenets of his philosophy, we shall see as we proceed.

2. Self-intuition, Primary and Basis of all other Knowledge.

Sankara's commentary on the *Upanishads*, the *Vedanta Sutras* and *Bhagavad-Gita* are the most important of his works and are the only ones that can, without doubt, be ascribed to him. These writings, as a matter of course, follow no system, or, if any, only that which the original works commented upon follow. This is one reason why the ordinary reader cannot understand Sankara. To make him intelligible, the main doctrines of his philosophy must be set down in something like a logical order and the arguments adduced by him in defence of each also set forth. We shall try something like this in the present account of his philosophy. We invite the reader, therefore, first of all, to grasp the very fundamental principle of Sankara's system—the primary nature of self-intuition (*asmatpratyaya* or *ahampratyaya*). In his commentary on the seventh aphorism of the third *pada*, second chapter, of the *Sariraka Mimamsa*, he says: "The self is not contingent in the case of any person; for it is self-evident. The self is not established by proofs of the existence of the self." Later on he says: "Nor is it possible to deny such a reality, for it is the very essence of him who would deny it." He then proceeds to show that this primary and self-evident intuition of self is the basis of all other kinds of knowledge, whether perceptive or inferential, direct or indirect, present, past or future. That is to say, we cannot know any object without knowing our self as the knower. As to the necessity or self-evident character of the proposition, "I know my self in knowing anything else," anyone may convince himself of this by trying to think its opposite, which will be found to be not only unthinkable, but actually self-contradictory. Thus, if it seems to the reader that while reading this book with deep attention he really forgets himself, he will find, on actual examination, that the proposition is really unthinkable and even absurd. He will see that if such a thing were possible, if he could really forget himself in reading this book, if he could, in other words, know it out of conscious relation to himself, it would not be possible afterwards to bring the object in relation to his consciousness, as he will actually do. Perhaps he will say that at one moment he actually knows the book, that is, sees or reads it, without knowing himself as the seer or reader, that is, without knowing that it is he who sees or reads it, but that at another moment he remembers that it was really he who read the book. But how is it possible for anyone to remember anything without actually knowing it? Remembering is recognition—knowing again—and there can be no recognition without cognition. To say, therefore, that one remembers anything without knowing it, is to say that one knows it without knowing it, which is absurd. If, in the present case, the reader says that he reads this book or any part of it without knowing his self as its reader, and then, at another time he remembers himself as its reader, he is really guilty of self-contradiction. Sankara's contention, therefore, that the knowledge of self is the constant basis of all other knowledge, is quite evident.

3. The World relative to Knowledge.

We now proceed to explain another cardinal doctrine of Sankara's philosophy,—the relativity of the world to knowledge. The ordinary unreflective reader has no suspicion of this relativity. To him the world exists whether anyone knows it or not. He constantly thinks and speaks of visible objects as existing unseen, audible objects as unheard, tangible things as untouched, and intelligible facts as unrelated to any understanding. He never suspects that such conceptions are self-contradictory and that the existence of an object necessarily implies the existence of a subject or knowing self in relation to whose knowledge it exists. If, as we have seen, we cannot know objects without knowing the self as its knower, it follows that we cannot *think* of any object without thinking of the same self as its knower; and if we must *believe* objects to exist exactly as they are known and thought of—and we cannot do otherwise—we must believe them existing as *known*—as the object of a knowing self. In other words, since we know objects as seen, heard, smelt, tasted, touched or understood,—as in some way or other related to the knowing self,—and can think of them only as so related,—therefore, to believe them as existing out of this relation is really to believe that things seen exist unseen, things heard exist unheard and so on, which is believing in contradictions as palpable as any can be. So Sankara says in his commentary on the *Prasnopanishad, VI.* 2: "It cannot be said that there exists an object, but it cannot be known. It is like saying that a visible object is seen, but there is no eye. . . . Where there is no knowledge there is no knowable. The fact is that in thinking of objects, all, whether they are reflective or unreflective, do think of a knowing self, but that unreflective people, because of their inability to analyse their thoughts, are not distinctly aware of this fundamental condition of all thought.

4. Self, the only Reality Known.

Now, from what has been said above it may seem that in knowing the world we know two distinct entities, namely, the self as the subject of knowledge, and Nature as the object of knowledge,—that though the existence of Nature implies its relation to a knowing self, it is nevertheless a distinct reality, and not identical with the self. But it will be seen on close examination that this distinction of Nature from the self is only apparent, not real. Sankara shows this clearly in his commentary on the first *anuvak* of the 'Brahmananda Valli' of the *Taittiriya Upanishad.* As he says there, "Appearances such as sound, though they present themselves as objects of self-knowledge, (and, therefore, as distinct from it) are yet found to be *pervaded by* self-knowledge." "The essence of the self," says he in the same commentary, "is knowledge, which can never be parted from it." If, then, every object is found to be pervaded by knowledge, the very essence of the self, no object can be distinct from the self, but is really comprehended in it. As a pleasure or a pain, though verbally distinguishable from the self which feels it, is really one with it, so are colours, tastes, smells, sounds and touches one with the self that perceives them, though they are verbally distinguishable from it. In knowing the world, therefore, we know nothing but the self. The distinction of subject and object is only conventional—*vyavaharika*, as Sańkara calls it—and the result of ignorance—*avidya*—ignorance which is removed by true knowledge. In every act of knowledge we know one, undivided entity—the self which is both subject and object, because it knows only itself and nothing else, or,—as the distinction of subject and object is only conventional—which is neither subject nor object, but transcends the distinction.

5. Space does not effect Duality. Between the Self and the World.

But our notion of the quality of subject and object, of the self and the world, is not likely to be given up unless the source of this notion is traced and shown to be unreliable. Its source, then, is time and space, the idea of which regulates all our sensuous perceptions. We shall consider space first and see how it breaks up, or rather seems to break up, the fundamental unity of consciousness. Space not only brings in the distinction of one object from another, but also that of the self from the world. The self seems to be *here*, in the body or in some particular part of the body, and the world, or any particular object in the world, *there*, out of the self. But this distinction of *in* and *out*, *here* and *there*, as between the self and the world, is the result of identifying the self with the body or some part of the body, and of forgetting that its essence is knowledge. As knowledge, the self is not only here, in a particular object, but everywhere, in all objects, for, as has already been seen, it pervades or illumines every thing it knows. As the *Kathopanishad, II.* 1. 10. says, and Sankara fully endorses, "What is here, is also there; what is there, is also here. He who sees duality in this, goes from death to death." Again, as the *Chhandogya*

Upanishad, VII. 15. 1. says and Sankara concurs, " The self alone is below, the self above, the self behind, the self before, the self to the right, the self to the left; the self is all this." The fact is that space, as an object of knowledge, is comprehended in the knowing self and cannot be out of it. The distinction of *here* and *there*, *in* and *out*, therefore, cannot subsist as between the self and its objects. For the self, there cannot be, in the proper sense of the term, any external object or world. The notion of an external or material world, therefore, is purely conventional,—*vyavaharika*— and is rejected by true knowledge. Space, which seems to make the Universe dual or plural, does not really do so. On the contrary, as a type of unity, it supplies Sankarâ with an illustration of the perfect oneness and indivisibility of the self. The distinction of *here* and *there*, of *this* and *that*, as between objects, does not, it will be seen, split up space itself into parts. The space inside a pot may seem to be different from that outside of it, but really there is no partition between the two. The walls or sides of the pot, which seem to part the inside space from the outside, are themselves in space, and, therefore, cannot part space from space. Similarly, the body, which seems to separate the self from the world, or the self in the body from the self in the world, does not really do so, for both the body and the world outside of it are illumined by the same self,—are objects of the same knowing self—and are thus comprehended in its essence. The notion of duality, therefore, as furnished by space, may be rejected as groundless. Objects, which seem to come to us as aliens, and as from a foreign source, are really one with what we call our self.

6. Knowledge really Non-sensuous, Unchangeable, and Eternal.

But if it be so, how is it, it may be urged, that objects do not always remain before or in the self, but seem to appear to it and disappear from it. If they were one with the self, would not they be ever present with it and the continual flux experienced in our perceptions be impossible? Sankara discusses the subject very fully in his introduction to the second chapter of the *Aitareya Upanishad* and, as the result of a long discussion, comes to the conclusion that the constant change apparent in our perceptions *does* not really imply any change in the knowledge of the self, in which all things exist eternally,—not, indeed, as objects distinguished from a subject, for the self transcends this distinction,—but in perfect unity with it. Our perceptions seem to result from the contact of our organs of knowledge with objects external to them. But real knowledge, as it is in the self, is not such a resultant. It is an eternal attribute of the self. In reality it neither arises from the action of external objects upon the senses nor is destroyed in the absence of such action. If it were so, says Sankara, there would not be such things as visions and sounds in the dreaming state, when the organs of perception are inactive. "Thus," he says, "there are two kinds of vision, that of the eye, which is transient, and that of the self, which is eternal. Similarly also two kinds of hearing, that of the ear, which is transient, and that of the self, which is eternal. Similarly two kinds of thought and knowledge, external and internal." That knowledge, though seeming to be in a flux, is really not so, but is a permanent property of the self, receives a striking illustration from the familiar but none the less wonderful fact of remembrance. The fact that things disappearing from the stream of changes that constitutes our sensuous life do yet re-appear and are recognised as identical with things known before, proves that knowledge is non-sensuous and does not depend for its existence on the changing and flowing from which it assumes in our perceptive life. Thus, if the knowledge of the book before me were a mere event, a change, a perceptive act, as it is called, it would vanish for ever on the cessation of the other actions, internal and external, on which it seems to depend,—my attention, the action of light on the eye, and the like. We should know nothing about it, at any rate, after a period of sound sleep, when all perceptive action ceases. But we know, as a fact, that it will re-appear to-morrow,—re-appear in relation with the self that now forms its ground and cause, and thereby prove itself as a permanent property of the self—as belonging to its very essence. It will prove that it was never absent from the knowledge of the self, —knowledge which, though different from sensuous knowledge, is none the less real than it, but rather infinitely more so. Sankara says all this in effect in his refutation of the Buddhist Sensationalism (*Kshanikavijnana-vada* in the second *pada* of the second chapter of the *Vedanta Sutras*. One short quotation from that long discussion must suffice after all that we have said on the subject. "Unless there exists," says Sankara, "one relating principle in the past, present and future—one which is unchangeable and sees all things—the facts of remembrance, recognition, &c., which depend upon mental impressions requiring space, time and occasional cause, cannot be explained."

7. UNREALITY OF TIME, SPACE AND THE FINITE SELF.

It is clear, then, from what has been said above, that in every act of knowledge we know only one Reality—that which we call our self —and that the objective world, the world of time and space, has no independent existence, but is comprehended in the self. The self alone has *paramarthika* or real existence, whereas the existence of the world is only *vyavaharika*, practical or phenomenal. The belief in its independent or real existence is the result of *avidya*, ignorance,—ignorance which is removed or destroyed by a true knowledge of reality. From the *paramarthika* standpoint there is no object as distinguished from the subject, no world, no space, no time; no action—therefore, and no agent, for action and agency depend on time. The argument for the unreality of space and time, which we have already given at some length, may be briefly summarised as follows: space is the distinction of *here* and *there*. The distinction obtains only as long as the principle that relates or unifies *here* and *there* is not seen, or, in other words, as long as object in space are believed to be realities independent of the self. When, however, *here* and *there* are both seen to be comprehended in the self—in that indivisible unity of consciousness, in which there is no distinction of *here* and *there*,—the distinction itself ceases to be real and with that ceases the reality of space. Similarly, time which is the distinction of *now* and *then*, ceases to be real when it is seen in relation to the self, for which the distinction has no existence; for, while present, past and future events go and come, the self persists and knows all. Even this going and coming of objects, is, as we have already seen, only apparent, and seems to be real only so long as objects are believed to be independent of the self. When they are seen to be identical with the self, it is found that they can neither go nor come, and we find, by actual experience, that facts disappearing from our perceptive life and apparently destroyed, re-appear in that life and prove their permanent, timeless existence in the self in its non-perceptive aspect. Now, as to the unreality of action and agency, they follow from what has been said as regards the unreality of space and time. Sankara indeed speaks, now and again, of knowledge as an action, as we too have done in expounding his doctrine. But according to him its character as an action, as a change or event, is only *vyavaharika*. As we have already said, it is only if you look upon objects or facts as different from the self that they seem to come and go, and the self seems to be an agent in the act of knowing. When this distinction is seen to be unreal, knowledge appears in its true character, namely, as the permanent essence of the self, and not a passing act or quality. Then, again, as to the perfect unity of the self, notwithstanding the fact that it appears different in different persons, the fact is evident from what we have already said. It is time and space and their various modifications that seem to break up the Universe into various parts, various spheres of knowledge and activity, and thus into different selves to which they are related. With the merging of time and space in the self, the idea of a plurality of selves is seen to be groundless. When the agencies that introduce finitude into reality are seen to be unreal, finitude itself disappears and the Infinite alone remains. Thus is our own self, the self in each of us, which we ignorantly imagine to be finite, seen to be really nothing but Brahman, *satyam-jnanamanantam*,—truth, knowledge and infinitude, or the True, the Knowing and the Infinite, if by these adjectives we understand a Reality of which truth, knowledge and infinitude are not separable attributes, but form its very essence. In his commentary on the first *anuvak* of the "Brahmananda Valli" of the *Taittiriya Upanishad*, Sankara discusses these attributes of Brahman at great length and shows that the terms expressing them are applied to Brahman in a sense somewhat different from what they bear in their application to phenomenal objects. They are used, in the case of Brahman, not to describe him,—for he cannot be described, as description implies distinction, and Brahman cannot be distinguished from anything other than he —but simply to indicate his nature as the one only Reality, self-illumined, self-dependent, indivisible and excluding even the possibility of any other reality. To the attributes already enumerated, is added *anandam*, bliss, not in the sense of the happiness experienced in obtaining a pleasurable object external to one's own self, but such happiness as a non-dual, secondless Reality can feel in the plenitude of its own nature.

8. Brahman as Isvara.

Having explained as fully as our limits allowed Sankara's idea of *paramarthika* existence, we proceed to give a fuller statement than we have hitherto done of the *vyavaharika* world as conceived by him. We see already that he does not pronounce the world of sensuous objects and finite selves as absolutely non-existent. Far from doing so, he rather admits that in one sense that world is as real as Brahman, for, in its real essence it is one with Brahman—comprehended in Brahman's indivisible essence. Sankara is never tired of repeating the *Chhandogya* text '*Sarvam khalu idam Brahma*'—Verily all this is Brahman. It is only the world's existence as conceived to be distinct from Brahman that is unreal according to him. Such a conception, he says, is based on ignorance and disappears on the attainment of true knowledge. Now, the question is whence is this ignorance—this fruitful source of the infinite variety that constitutes the world? In reply, Sankara has no hesitation in saying that this potent agency belongs to Brahman himself, though in saying so he seems to contradict himself palpably. Is not Brahman, as conceived by Sankara, the very essence of knowledge? How, then, could there be ingorance in him even for a single moment? Is not Sankara's Brahman a non-agent (*nishkriya*)? How, then, could any power or agency belong to him? We confess we find no clear answers to such questions in Sankara. His oft-repeated answer is that *avidya* is *anirvachaniya*, not clearly describable, for it cannot be said to be either one with Brahman or different from him. In its effect, as manifested in the life of a being conceived as finite, *avidya*, indeed, is not indescribable. It can very well be described as the finite self's ignorance of its own true nature, removable by true knowledge, as Sankara does describe it now and again, for instance, in his commentary on the third aphorism of the fourth *pada*, first chapter, of the *Vedanta Sutras*. The indescribability comes in when it is asked, how could there be any room for a finite being, or—what is practically the same thing—for the conception of such a being in a Reality infinite and without the least shade of distinction? Fully recognising this indescribableness, however, Sankara finds himself committed to the postulation of a power, dependent on Brahman and called indifferently *Avidya* or *Maya*, which gives rise to subjects and objects phenomenally but not absolutely real. This power does not, indeed, make Brahman either ignorant or limited, for he is independent of, and therefore untouched by, it. But as related to it, he assumes a character which does not belong to him as conceived apart from it. This 'assumption' is not indeed an affair of time, not anything that begins to be at one time, and ceases to be at another, for, though the effects of *Maya* come and go, *Maya* itself, as a power, is eternal. But nevertheless, as it is a power producing unreal appearances, Sankara refuses to ascribe to it *paramarthika* or absolute existence. However, in relation to this power, Brahman is Isvara, the Ruler,—the Creator, Preserver and Destroyer of the world,—all-knowing, all-powerful, merciful, just, holy, the friend and saviour of finite souls. As Isvara, then, Brahman has all the chracteristics of what is called a Personal God. Sankara's views on *Maya* and Isvara will be found explained at some length in his commentary on the fourteenth aphorism of the first *pada*, second chapter, of the *Vedanta Sutras*, besides other passages. We make no quotations, as detached passages on the matter are not likely to convey any clear idea. The eternality and indestructibleness of *Maya* will be found admitted in the commentary on the *Vedanta Sutras*, I. 1. 5 and II. 1. 9.

9. THE COSMIC SOUL AND THE COSMOS. BONDAGE AND LIBERATION.

With the personality of Brahman at the top of the *vyavaharika* world, Sankara gives back all that he seems to have taken away by his process of merging everything finite in the Infinite. With the Creator he gives back the world created and sustained by him, with all the finite objects and finite souls contained in it, and he sharply criticises the Buddhist Sensationalists for denying their existence, in the same manner in which he takes the Sankhya philosophers to task for their rejecting the most rational doctrine of an intelligent Creator of the world in favour of their unintelligent Prakriti. At the head of all created beings he places the *Karya* or *Apara* Brahman, the Effect-God or Lower Brahman, as distinguished from God as Cause or the Higher, Supreme Brahman. He is otherwise called Brahma or Hiranyagarbha. As objects can exist only in relation to and in distinction from a subject, as changes imply a mind of which they are modifications, the objective world as a totality implies the existence of a Subject to which it is related,—a Mind of which all cosmic changes are modifications. This Mind considers the world as its body, just as individual minds consider smaller aggregates of objects as their bodies. This Lower Brahman is *saguna*, *i. e.*, immanent in *sattvam*, *rajas* and *tamas*, the primary *gunas* or qualities of Nature, and their innumerable modifications; whereas the Supreme Brahman is *nirgunam*, without the *gunas*, *i.e.*, transcending the qualities of Nature. Under Brahma, and comprehended in his all-pervading life, are the various classes of individual beings such as gods, demons, men and the lower animals. All are, indeed, one with Brahman in essence, but they appear finite and distinct from him in consequence of their indentifying themselves with certain aggregates of objects which they consider as their bodies or limiting adjuncts (*upadhis*). These aggregates, in the ascending order of their subtlety, are the following five:—(1) the nutritive or material sheath (*annamaya kosha*), (2) the vital sheath (*pranamaya kosha*), (3) the sensorial sheath (*manomaya kosha*), (4) the intellectual sheath (*vijnanamaya kosha*) and (5) the beatific sheath (*anandamaya kosha*). These aggregates are called sheaths (*koshas*), for they keep the real nature of the self hidden, just as the sheath enclosing a sword keeps it hidden. The soul, in the lowest stage of its spiritual development, identifies itself with the body composed of gross matter ; in the next stage with the vital powers ; then with the sensorium *manas*, the seat of sensations ; then with the intellect or understanding, the faculty that forms general conceptions and leads us to imagine ourselves as agents and subjects of knowledge ; and then ultimately with delightful feelings of all classes, specially the higher. But when enlightenment dawns upon us, we discover the truth that these aggregates, as limited objects, are not our real self, and are not limiting adjuncts to it. Our real self, we find, is infinite and absolute—the Supreme Brahman himself. Our self-identification with a limited object, with all its sin and misery is our bondage, while the consciousness of unity with Brahman, with all the holiness and blessedness pertaining to such consciousness,, is our liberation. The subject of the five sheaths and our identification with and liberation from them, the reader will find treated of in Sankara's commentary on the 'Brahmananda Valli' and the 'Bhrigu Valli' of the *Taittiriya Upanishad.*

10. Incarnation, Universal and Special.

We now come to a consideration of the means proposed by Sankara for obtaining liberation and the processes through which, according to him, the soul obtains it. But before entering into a proper discussion of these subjects, we shall briefly notice Sankara's view of incarnation, both because it is an important doctrine of speculative philosophy and because it is closely connected with Sankara's view of ethical and spiritual life. It must be clear from what we have already said that Sankara holds a doctrine which may be called that of universal incarnation. Every so-called finite being is, according to him, an incarnation of the Deity, inasmuch as the self we call our own is realy the Supreme Self. It is only our ignorance that hides our identity with Brahman, and this ignorance is quite removable by knowledge. When this ignorance is removed, we realise the truth of the *mahavakyas*, great utterances, of the Vedanta—'*So'ham*' ((*Isopanishad*, 16)—I am He, '*Aham Brahmasmi*' (*Brihadaranyaka*, I. 4, 10.)—I am Brahman, and '*Tattvam asi*' (*Chhandogya*, vi. 8.)—Thou art That,—utterances which Sankara is never tired of repeating. Nevertheless, this identity of God and man, however real and essential, has to be discovered through a process in the case of the ordinary individual. The question now is, is there, or has there ever been, any individual in whom the consciousness of identity with the Deity is eternal and not discoverable through a process? In other words, has God ever incarnated himself—manifested himself as an individual like ourselves, with body, sensorium and understanding like ours? It is curious that Sankara has nowhere, in his writings, discussed this question philosophically—setting forth the arguments in favour of and against this doctrine of special incarnation. But it is evident from several passages in his work, specially from the introduction to his commentary on the *Bhagavad-Gita*, that he accepts the popular doctrine of Sri Krishna, son of Devaki, being the incarnation of the Deity in a special sense. But in the particular passage referred to, he uses a word which seems considerable to differentiate his view of the Divine incarnation from the popular view. He says that in Devaki as mother and from Vasudeva as father, the Creator '*Amsena Krishnah kila sambabhuva*'—was born *in part* as Krishna. One can see very well why Sankara uses the word *amsena*, in part, in speaking of the Lord's incarnation. Incarnation is manifestation in flesh and other mediums like the sensorium and the understanding, which are all finite things. Now, the manifestation of the Self through finite things cannot but be partial, and so Sri Krishna, however superior he may have been to ordinary mortals, would yet seem to have been a finite being so far as his manifested or perceptive life was concerned. But if it be so, it is not easy to see what difference *in kind* exists between him and other individuals. Sankara, however, never distinctly makes the admission to which he seems to be committed and, excepting the reservation implied in the word *amsena*, everywhere speaks of Sri Krishna as the incarnation of the Lord in a special sense. It may be mentioned by the way that the doctrine of special incarnation is absent from the *Upanishads*—the twelve that form the basis of the Vedanta Philosophy—and from the *Vedanta Sutras*.

11. Admissions inconsistent with Absolute Monism.

However, Sankara's acceptance of the doctrine of special incarnation commits him to two very important admissions,—admissions which seem to conflict with the general drift of his philosophy. The first is that the state of absolute liberation does not imply an utter annihilation of difference; in that state also, as in the state of bondage, there is a recognition of the plurality that constitutes the world,—only, that recognition is coupled with the consciousness that plurality is *mayik*, the result of the Lord's mysterious power of creation. To Sri Krishna himself, the incarnation of the eternally free Lord, moving among the Kurus and the Pandavas, driving the chariot of his friend and pupil in the battle-field, and instructing him in the supreme science of liberation, there is evidently a distinct recognition of all the differences that constitute the phenomenal world, including his own distinction, as the Universal Self, from other persons as finite individuals. We shall see hereafter how far Sankara keeps this admission in view in his distinction of *karma* or *apekshiki mukti* (gradual or relative liberation) and *para* or absolute liberation. The second admission referred to above is that even liberated—absolutely liberated—souls may re-incarnate themselves, not indeed under the influence of desires, or as the result of past actions, for all desires and fruits of action are dead in their case, but for the object of doing good to the world,—liberating those who are still in bondage. This admission also Sankara seems now and again to nullify by his doctrine of the final merging of individual souls in Brahman and that of the essential opposition of *karma* (action) and liberation.

12. The Four Gatis or Destinies, the Opposition of Jnana and Karma.

We come, therefore, to a consideration of Sankara's view of *karma*. According to him there are four stages of spiritual progress, and accordingly, as one occupies one or another of these stages at the time of one's death, he obtains one or another of four corresponding *gatis*, fates or conditions, in the period following his departure from the world. In his commentary on the *Chhandogya Upanishad*, V. 10, *Brihadaranyaka*, VI. 2, and elsewhere he speaks of these four stages and the fates to which they lead. The lowest is that in which man—and what is said of man applies to other orders of being also—does not subject himself to any Vedic discipline, but lives a life of pure impulse unchecked by any higher law. Such men, when they die, are reborn in the form of some lower animal such as a fly or an insect. The next higher stage is that in which man performs the duties prescribed in the *Srutis* and the *Smritis*, but acquires no knowledge regarding the gods he worships. The highest reward allotted to this stage is the attainment of the lunar regions through the way called the *pitriyana*—the path of the manes—and the enjoyment, for a time, of the joys provided there. When these are over, with the exhaustion of the enjoyer's *punya* or merit,—which, however great, is nevertheless a perishable thing,—he comes down and is re-born. The third higher stage is that in which the performer of *karma* prescribed in the Scriptures adds to his virtuous deeds a knowledge of the deities worshipped by him. The deities spoken of in this connection do not include the Supreme Deity, the Highest Brahman. The highest god known in his stage is the Apara-Brahman or Hiranyagarbha. He is known and worshipped as distinct from the worshipper, at least in some respects, and it is the consciousness of his distinction from the object of his worship that makes it possible for him to worship it and to seek his own good in various finite shapes by sacrifices to the gods and the performances of other duties prescribed in the Scriptures. The highest reward assigned to this stage is the attainment of the Divine regions—*Brahma-loka*—through the *devayana* or the path of the gods. When this world has once been attained, there is no return from it to lower worlds. The soul lives there for ages in the company of the gods and in close proximity to the Lower Brahman, and when this Brahman himself is merged in the Highest Brahman at the end of the cycle (kalpa), his worshippers also share in his happy fate.* This process of obtaining liberation is called by Sankara *karma-mukti*—gradual liberation. As the attainment of the *Brahmaloka* is itself called *mukti* in the *Srutis* and the *Sutras*, San-

* See Saukara's commentary on the *Prasnopanishad*, *VI*. 5, and that on the *Vedanta Sutras*, *IV*. 3.

kara calls this state *apekshiki-mukti*—relative liberation. We see, then, how far, according to Sankara, *karma* alone—the mere performance of prescribed duties—on the one hand, and *karma* coupled with *apara vidya*, the lower knowledge,—the knowledge of the gods—on the other, can take us. Beyond all such finite forms of personal good (*purushartha*) lies *para-mukti*, absolute liberation, which consists in perfect union with the Supreme Being without a single shade of difference. This can be secured only by the *para vidya jnana*—the knowledge of one's perfect identity with Para-Brahman. When this knowledge is acquired, the soul is in no need of making a journey through the *devayana* to the *Brahmaloka*. It becomes *jivan-mukta*, liberated though living in the world, and is at death, completely merged in Brahman. The *jnana* which secures *jivan-mukti* is, according to Sankara, incompatible with *karma* of all sorts. Such *jnana* shows the identity of the self with the Supreme Brahman, who is, as we have already seen, a non-agent, *akarta*, and is above all needs and, therefore, all desires. How can one who knows oneself to be the eternally complete Brahman have any motive for action? Hence Sankara fights a long and interminable battle against *Samuchchayavada*, the doctrine of the union of *jnana* and *karma*. According to the upholders of this doctrine, both knowledge and action are necessary for liberation, and even those who have attained the highest knowledge should perform the duties prescribed in the Scriptures, though without any selfish desires. The life of a householder, therefore, is not, according to these theorists, incompatible with the highest knowledge. Sankara admits that the performance of the duties prescribed in the Sriptures is necessary for purifying the heart, and that, unless the heart is purified, the highest knowledge cannot be attained. But he thinks that when the necessary purification of the heart has taken place, and the highest knowledge has arisen, ceremonial and domestic duties, that is *karma* in the proper sense, become unnecessary, and the only duties that remain then are those that ripen and strengthen the knowledge of Brahman. Of this latter class of duties we shall give Sankara's views further on. Against the former, and against the life of a housholder, which is based on them, Sankara speaks everywhere throughout his writings. But we may refer to two particular passages as containing a summary of his views on the subject. His refutation of *Samuchchayavada* will be found specially in his commentary on the eleventh verse of the second chapter of the *Bhagavad-Gita*, which is really the opening note of the commentary, coming immediately after the introduction. His advocacy of *sannyasa*, the ascetic's life, as the only one compatible with the highest knowledge, and his tirade against the householder's life as inconsistent with the knowledge of Brahman, will be found specially in his introduction to the commentary on the *Aitareya Upanishad*. In the first-mentioned commentary, however, he makes an admission which seems to be a virtual surrender of his position. Herein he says that the performance of a *kshatriya's* duties by Sri Krishna, the incarnation of the Lord, for the good of the world, and of ceremonial and domestic duties by Janaka and other householders who had gained the highest knowledge, with the same object, was not such *karma* as he (Sankara) teaches to be incompatible with the highest knowledge. The absence of desire (*kama*) and egotism (*ahankara*) in such actions takes them away from the category of *karma* properly so called. After this concession, very little, if any, difference remains between Sankara's position and that of the *Samuchchayavadin*, specially if the latter accepts, in their entirety, the teachings of the *Gita* on disinterested action (*nishkama karma*).

13. Re-incarnation. Relative and Absolute Liberation.

We must return, however, to the four different *gatis* or destinies to which, in the opinion of Sankara, the soul becomes subject according to its behaviour on earth. All of them, it will be seen, imply a belief in re-incarnation. Sankara offers no regular philosophical defence of the tenet of re-incarnation, though it is easy to see, from his writings, what arguments he would have adduced in favour of the doctrine if he had been called upon to argue it out. We, therefore, attempt neither any defence nor any criticism of the theory. The reader, if he feels any curiosity about it, may consult the section on 'Re-incarnation' in the present writer's treatise on *Hindu Theism*, where he will find the doctrine defended at some length with arguments both old and new. For our present purpose, it will be sufficient to say that there is nothing, *prima facie*, irrational and, therefore, unphilosophical in the ideal of re-incarnation. The immortality of the soul being admitted, the next question is whether an embodied or a disembodied existence is the more probable form of the soul's continuance in after-life, a question the settlement of which will depend upon the weight of arguments on either side. But the same rationality can scarcely be urged in favour of Sankara's doctrine that souls not subject to any discipline in this life will be re-born in the shape of some lower animal. The conception of such a destiny for a human being seems to ignore the vast difference between the human consciousness and that of the lower animals. Even the most degraded of human beings seem to be incomparably superior to the lower animals, and though a process of progression, by which higher orders of being are developed out of the lower, is a rational idea, defensible both scientifically and philosophically, a reverse process of retrogression seems opposed to both science and philosophy. The first of the four *gatis* spoken of by Sankara, thus seems to be philosophy indefensible. Coming, now, to the second and the third, the soul's passage to the *Pitriloka* and the *Brahmaloka*, we must say that these doctrines scarcely come under the category of philosophical, since they are not defended by arguments, but are put forward as interpretations of Scriptural texts. There is, indeed, nothing intrinsically irrational in the idea of an abode of the virtuous like the *Pitriloka*, though there seems to be something mechanical in that of one's merit being exhausted there in time and necessitating a fall and re-birth. There is, also, nothing unreasonable, in itself, in the idea of a world occupied by the higher gods, that is of the most wise and holy of finite beings, where the Divine presence, though pervading the whole universe is felt most vividly, and imparts a blessedness which cannot be enjoyed anywhere else. But nevertheless Sankara's teachings about such a world and the way by which the soul reaches it, rest on no better or higher authority than the utterances of the Scriptures and must be accepted or rejected according to the light in which we regard these authorities. It may also be doubted whether Scriptural teaching on this subject is at all to be taken in a literal sense,—as treating of an actual world and an actual way—or is altogether figurative—representing a spiritual condition as a world, and a process of spiritual progress as a way. A careful study of the *Kaushitaki Upanishad*, Chapter I., *Chhandogya, IV. 15*, and *Brihadaranyaka, VI. 2. 15*, which contain accounts of the *Brahmaloka*, its contents, and the way to it, does really suggest such a doubt. Sankara, however, and the other interpreters of the *Srutis*, including the author of the *Vedanta Sutras*, interpret these descriptions as realistic. But there is a curious difference among these interpreters as to one important point, a consideration of which will lead us to the discussion of the fourth *gati* spoken of by Sankara, namely, the union of the soul with the Supreme Brahman, which is the only one that admits of philosophical discussion in the proper sense of the term. The difference referred to is whether the Brahman approached by the *devayana* is the higher or the lower Brahman. Two ancient interpreters of the Scriptures, Jaimini and Badari, take opposite sides. According to the former, it is the higher Brahman that is reached by the way ; according to the latter it is the lower. The difference is into a mere difference of textrial interpretation: it leads to important philosophical differences, and hence our taking it up in this book. The author of the *Sutras* simply mentions the views of the ancient interpreters, with their arguments, side by side, but does not clearly take any side. Sankara, however, thinks that he takes Badari's side, whereas Ramanuja, the great Vaishnava philosopher, and a great opponent of Sankara's philosophy, interprets the author of the Sutras as in favour of Jaimini's view. It would perhaps be preposterous for us to take any side when such great authorities find reason to differ; nor is it necessary for us to do so. The fact, however, is that the soul's union with Brahman in the *Brahmaloka*, which is described in the scriptural passages already referred to, and in the last three *padas* of the fourth Chapter of the *Vedanta-Sutras*, is a union with several points of difference. The soul sees its essential unity with Brahman, but neither obtains all the powers of the Deity nor is completely merged in it. The author of the *Sutras* distinctly calls this condition liberation, and the Vaishnava philosophers hold it to be the highest condition attainable by a finite being. Hence also they interpret it as union with the highest Brahman, between whom and a finite being there must always exist, as they teach, some points of difference. But Sankara thinks that as Para-Brahman is above all difference, the soul's union with him must be a condition without a shadow of difference (*bheda*) in it, and he finds scriptural authority for such a condition in such passages as the seventh verse, fourth section, fourth chapter of the *Brihadaranyaka Upanishad.* It is not easy to conceive what Sankara precisely means by such a condition. His oft-repeated characterisation of it as one without the least vestige of difference would seem to make it incompatible even with the consciousness that all differences are *mayik*, or phenomenal. But if we were to interpret it in the light of admissions as to the eternality and indestructibility of *Maya* or the principle of difference, and as to Sri Krishna, the

Lord's incarnation, and liberated souls working for the good of the world, and thus being conscious of phenomenal differences, then we should have to conceive even absolute liberation as admitting of a sort of differentiation—though it were a differentiation very dissimilar to that which the soul conceives under the influence of *avidya*. Notwithstanding the difficulty of an exact interpretation of Sankara on the point, we lean towards the view that it is the latter kind of differentiation, and not the former, that he is careful of excluding from his conception of absolute liberation. However, the absolutely liberated soul does not, according to Sankara, need to go anywhere in particular, and through any way, to obtain its highest condition. It becomes the Supreme Brahman himself, who is in all space and time, or,—what is really the same thing,—beyond all space and time. It becomes so even while living in the body. But Sankara makes a difference, as will be seen from his interpretation of the texts referred to above, between having a body and being freed from it, and seems to think that liberation is not quite complete till the body is dissolved. This distinction, again, seems to conflict with his definition of liberation as the attainment of the highest knowledge,—which can have nothing to do with the dissolution of a physical organism—and with the admission that the incarnation of the eternally free Lord and other liberated souls lived and moved in bodies without the least prejudice to their freedom.

14. Bhakti or Reverential Love to God.

We have seen now what place Sankara gives to *jnana* and *karma* in spiritual culture. It remains to be seen what he conceives to be the function of *bhakti* the reverential love of God, in the attainment of liberation. His commentary on the *Bhagavad Gita*, where *bhakti* is extolled now and again, leaves no doubt as to the high place it occupies in his system. In the *Vivekachudamani*, a beautiful treatise ascribed to him, he says: "Of the things which help the attainment of liberation, *bhakti* is the greatest"—'*Mokshakarana samagryam bhaktireva gariyasi.*' But it must be clear, both from the verse quoted and from the foregoing exposition of Sankara's view, that *bhakti* in the popular sense, as a feeling of reverence for a being conceived as higher than the soul of the devotee, can be regarded only as a help, a stepping-stone, to liberation in a system of Absolute Monism like Sankara's. And this is exactly the light in which Sankara regards it: it is a means, not the end,—a lower and not the final stage in the soul's progress. But there are passages in the *Bhagavad-Gita*, for instance, verses 54 and 55 of the eighteenth chapter, where the final stage of spiritual progress is described and yet *bhakti* finds a place there. How does Sankara interpret such passages? In such passages he simply takes *bhakti* as identical with *jnana* and he finds scriptural authority for so regarding it. In chapter VII, verse 16 of the *Gita*, Sri Krishna speaks of four classes of worshippers, and by implication, of four species of *bhakti*, and gives superiority to that which is identical with or based on *jnana*. *Jnana*, to Sankara, is the knowledge of the soul's identity with Brahman ; the highest form of *bhakti*, therefore, is the most constant and vivid consciousness of such identity. The other kinds of *bhakti* enumerated in the above text are the reverential feelings that inspire (1) those in distress, (2) those who desire knowledge, and (3) those whose object is to attain some particular end. Evidently Sankara would class even the highest dualistic *bhakti* under the second or third head.

15. Scheme of Spiritual Exercises.

Now, this leads us naturally to the subject of *upasanas* or devotional exercises, with a notice of which we shall close our account of Sankara's philosophy. In Sankara's scheme of spiritual exercises, a scheme which we have simply mentioned above, but have not given in detail, *upasana* comes under *samadhana*. The scheme is called *sadhana-chatushtaya*, the fourfold discipline. It comprises (1) *Nityanitya-vastu-viveka*, the discrimination of things permanent and transitory ; (2) *Ihamutra-phalabhoga-viraga* non-attachment to rewards of actions, earthly or heavenly; (3) *Samadamadi-sadhanasampat*, disciplines beginning with *sama* and *dama*; and (4) *Mumukshutvam*, desire for liberation. The discipline classed under the third head are *sama*, the drawing away of the mind from things earthly; *dama*, the restraining of the external senses; *uparati*, giving up, for the sake of obtaining the higher knowledge, the duties prescribed in the lower code; *titiksha*, patiently bearing the sufferings caused by heat, cold, &c.; *samadhana*, the concentration of the mind in higher things by giving up sleepiness and laziness; and *sraddha*, faith in all (higher) things. The reader will find these disciplines enumerated in Sankara's commentary on the first aphorism of the *Vedanta Sutras* and their meanings explained in the annotations of Govindananda, whom we have followed in he explanation we have given. The subject of *upasanas* he will find dealt with in the introduction to the commentary on the *Chhandogya Upanishad*, the greater portion of which is taken up with various kinds of devotional exercises. These Sankara divides into two broad classes: (1) those which are closely related to Vedic ceremonies and gradually lead the mind to higher exercises; and (2) those which, through the contemplation of Brahman in relation to the objects of Nature, both gross and subtle, lead us to a knowledge of him as transcendent,—to that highest form of knowledge in which all distinctions of subject and object, of action, agent and the result of action are merged in one, infinite, indivisible Entity.

16. Conclusion.

We take leave here of our great philosopher. Our object has been to expound rather than criticise his system. But we have suggested certain difficulties in it—such as no systems, ancient or modern, are entirely free from. Probably no ancient system will quite suit the modern mind. But we may perhaps be allowed to hazard the opinion that, of all ancient systems, that of Sankaracharya will be found to be the most congenial and the most easy of acceptance to the modern Indian mind.